It had promised to be a pretty peaceful Saturday. Early summer. All the kids were either outside playing or sleeping in. And then came Karen. Karen had blue eyes; at least that's what you thought at first glance. But then she stared at you, or you at her, and you realized there was a mother-lode of gold in her eyes, scattered around her irises like nuggets resting at the bottom of two sunlit pools. Unless she was mad. And then the gold seemed to shrink away. As if something stirred the gravel at the bottom of the pools and clouded the usual crystal clearness of her eyes. Believe me, no one, especially me, ever wanted to see that contrast between brightest sunlight and darkest shadow. Something inside me shrunk away in terror from the shadows in Karen's eyes.

"Mom,— Mom,— Mom,— ." She kept beginning and faltering. Something in her voice was different. New. No, old. She sounded like the little girl I'd known before the chasm opened up between us. She sounded like the little girl I had been before the chasm opened up in me to protect me from what no child should ever have to know.

"Mom,—" She paused again. Now she wasn't gasping for breath. Instead, she seemed frozen in the middle of a breath, terrified of the words her lips were forming. Something inside me *knew* why she paused: she was sure that if she used this breath to tell this truth, she would never breathe again. I have often thought, since, of the little boy who gave blood to save his sister's life, convinced he would die from the act. Karen was about to risk her life for my sake. To kill the lie in me.

—from *An Imperative Duty*

"Karl," I heard someone say. "Please, hold me." I stumbled off the bottom step and Brother Dunn put his arms around me. ... I stared over his shoulder at the stars beginning to appear in the evening sky. My soul felt like a computer on search, scanning the entire universe. Where was she? Where was my child? She wasn't gone. She couldn't be. She had to be somewhere under those same stars.

I couldn't comprehend that for over four hours now, I had been in the world, while she was not. I had gone on breathing, eating, talking, laughing, worrying over bills. ... Shouldn't a pit have formed in my stomach four hours ago? Shouldn't I have felt at least a twinge of nausea as she died? Shouldn't it have felt like someone was peeling away a piece of my soul? Shouldn't a shiver have gone down my spine as she passed? You know, like they show in the movies. I mean, even Lassie has more sensitivity, more intuition. I mean she *knows* when there's even a quiver in the fabric of her loved ones' lives.

But not me. No, not me.

—from *Train Up a Child*

A Voice from the Fire

The Authority of Experience

Colleen C . Harrison

WINDHAVEN
PUBLISHING & PRODUCTIONS
PLEASANT GROVE, UTAH

PUBLISHED BY:

PUBLISHING & PRODUCTIONS

PO BOX 282

PLEASANT GROVE, UT 84062

WWW.WINDHAVENPUBLISHING.COM

Printed in the United States of America

Cover Art: ©2002, Julie Ann Allen. Used with permission.
Cover Design and Typesetting: Professional Pre-Press, Pleasant Grove, Utah.

ISBN: 1–930738–16–1

This book is a collection of memoiristic essays based on the life experiences of the author. Names have been changed and some of the descriptions of places and events have been altered to offer anonymity to both the innocent and the guilty.

For all my children—

whoever they may be.

Acknowledgements

Having seen many afflictions in the course of my days, nevertheless, having been highly favored of the Lord in *all* my days, having a great knowledge of the *goodness* and mysteries of God—the greatest mystery being an absolute witness that if we will be patient with Him, He will work *all things* together for our good—I thus acknowledge His hand in all things:

> —in *all* my children, they are the jewels in my crown;

> —in *both* my husbands, the contrast between bitter and sweet is beyond expression;

> —in *all* my friends, for they have been the hands of the Lord to comfort and to teach;

> —in *all* my enemies, for they have been His instruments to chasten and purify me, and examples of the truth that wickedness never was happiness.

Table of Contents

$\mathcal{S}$ hakespeare once compared all the world to a stage and all the men and women in it to mere players. I prefer to compare life to a novel—a Dickens style novel (which by the way, I did not enjoy in high school)—long and complicated, with a plot that ebbs and flows so often you feel dizzy trying to keep up with it. You feel like you're drowning in the mundane details of your life. And then without warning, you are crushed in those conversely breath-taking, heart-wrenching scenes, when decision or destiny shatters the reverie of routine and causes such a divide that all the watershed of life, past and future, runs down hill from it. And the characters (including yourself) are puzzling, and sometimes perverse, with so many unpredictable strengths and weaknesses. And there are the combinations of interpersonal relationships—each person, each relationship, representing a simultaneous story, spinning out parallel to and yet intricately (and often confusingly) interwoven into each other's design until you want to scream and throw the book against the wall and be done with it forever,...but you can't, not without committing suicide. And tomorrow *is* another day—who knows what adventures may come.

*I*n the midst of the fiery moments of suffered and survived experience, I find myself able to testify with the power and the authority of *living* and *loving* Truth.

*A*nd for good measure, like the grains of sand poured in among the larger stones to fill a cup of love, a few poems.

I am a daughter of a Heavenly Father who loves me, and I love Him. I will stand as a witness of God at all times and in all things and in all places.

This is not idle rhetoric for me. I believe it absolutely, live by it absolutely—or as absolutely as a mortal human being can. When I pledge to stand as a witness of God, I stand as a witness of the *truth*, at all times, in all things, in all places. When we take the witness stand, we swear to tell "the truth, the whole truth, and nothing but the truth, so help me God." With this book as my witness stand, I swear to let my voice be heard. I swear to share my experiences, my learnings, my *truth* with as many as will listen. *My* truth—the truth *about me, my life*—the *whole* truth, and nothing but the truth. For this reason I pray, *"So, help me, God."*

A Voice from the Fire

The Authority of Experience

My heart was hot within me, while I was musing the fire burned.

—*Psalms 39:3*

A victim is a martyr without a voice. A martyr is a victim that has found her voice. Exquisite pain becomes exquisite joy when Truth is loved and spoken in plainness and humility. It is my prayer that the only Muse I trust, even the Spirit of Truth, will possess me in this work, be with me in the fire and transform the fires of martyrdom for both me and my children into the fires of exaltation.

For this purpose I cry from the fire.

Preface

A job! You've never held a *job* in your life. You need to get one. You can't live on your ex-husband's "charity" forever. You need to earn your own way, sooner or later, you know. You need to do something *practical* with your degree."

These were the thoughts sitting heavy on my mind as I received my Bachelors Degree in English at the age of forty-six. It was all true. I was a single mother of twelve, with sole custody of five children under the age of eighteen as I received my diploma that beautiful June day in 1994.

I could hardly believe I had achieved this dream—a dream put on hold nearly three decades earlier when I married at the age of eighteen. I always knew I would go back to school someday, but I thought it would be for "fun," when our children were grown and I was left with time to relax. It didn't happen that way. Even though I spent those twenty-three years believing in the ideal and slogging through the "reality" of being a stay-at-home mom, it all came crashing down around me on that other June morning, three years ago. In just ten minutes, my "for time and all eternity" marriage ran out of time. In ten minutes by the courtroom clock, my social and economic status changed 180 degrees. Suddenly I wasn't Colleen…, wife of…

I was "just" Colleen. Forty-two years old. Twenty-three years at home. Twelve children; eight still at home to feed, clothe, house, discipline and raise—alone. High school education plus two semesters of twenty-three-year-old college credits. Zero marketable skills. Income: from over $50,000 annually to under $20,000.

Still, I went through with the divorce.

It didn't matter to me whether I was jumping out of the proverbial frying pan and into the proverbial fire or not. The mixture of ingredients in the "pan"—in my "whited sepulcher" of a marriage—finally reached such a level of trauma that all my fears of poverty, of being on state welfare made no difference. I gave up my rigid interpretation of the LDS axiom, "Families are Forever." If mine was going to be a "forever family," it was going to have to be forever *for real*, without the pretense and false facade of "fineness" we lived behind for so long. For years I had turned the ideal of eternal marriage into idolatry. I put maintaining the appearance of marriage ahead of integrity, before respect of human life, including my own, before gospel principles, before concern for my children's well-being—before everything—even before family. It may sound crazy to some but, the truth was, my marriage was destroying any semblance of "family."

As I stood in the entrance tunnel to the subterranean floor of the Marriott Center, only moments from hearing my name announced to signal my procession through the handshakes, congratulations, smiles, and pictures of commencement, I thought of yet another June when Karen, my oldest daughter, graduated from high school in this very same setting. I looked up at the rows and rows of seats in the cavernous arena, stretching upwards hundreds of feet into the shadows at the top of the building. At the level of the rotunda, sunlight barely penetrated, silhouetting the tiny profiles of people as they came and went. From that distance there was no sound of their movements. They appeared less than an inch tall.

My eyes searched the thousands of faces of the people already seated. What if Karen was among them? What if she got "permission" to be here? What if it was all a mistake—the weekend she died? What if it was all a dream and this was the moment I was going to wake up? Far up in the sea of faces, I saw a form so familiar—at least similar. Someone waving wildly, blond-hair flashing. I pretended it was her and waved back. Someone yelled, "Go, Mom!" I let it be her. It would have been her. What if it *was* her? I mean, what about movies like *Ghost* and *Heart and Souls*. Come on. We love to believe.

She was dressed in a white cap and gown on her graduation day, replete with golden tassel that bounced and flounced with her jubilant movements. She was an angel-colored kite about to take off on a high wind. Even the heavy, almost garish lei of red and yellow flowers her best friend bought her didn't detract from her buoyancy and the brilliance of her flashing smile. I remember her, cheering and waving as she walked across the dais. I remember hundreds of friends cheering her. Everyone knew Karen. Everyone loved Karen.

I smiled at the memory and checked the half-dozen hair pins holding my cap in place. I wasn't nearly as young and brave and uninhibited as she had been. "Come on, Mom! Strut your stuff! You've earned it!" I could hear exactly what she would have said, if she could have. And maybe she did say it. Maybe those were her words, allowed into my mind by a loving and benevolent God. Tears welled up in my eyes. I was next. The sound of my name resounded through the air in the deep resonant tones of the announcer. "Rose CALL-een…" I spelled it that way on the card I filled out earlier, so it would be pronounced according to my Irish heritage and not "Co-leen," the more common pronunciation. I walked out into the light, up the stairs, receiving handshakes and congratulations and a temporarily empty diploma cover. I heard several of my other children cheering for me and in their tone, a touch of Karen's voice. It was enough.

On the hot August evening when Karen died, less than three short months after her high school graduation, she was into alcohol and drug use, running from the insanity perpetrated on her by both of her parents and their own more covert, socially acceptable addictions. The circumstances of her death sealed my testimony that the Lord Jesus Christ would stand with me through anything—no matter how "hot" the "fire" burned. I was also convinced of the truth that I could no longer live the lie—pretending things were not "that bad" in our family system.

For two years following Karen's death, I remained in the marriage, pleading with my husband to own our terrible private failure within our home. Finally, the day came that it was over. I had no more hope or stamina to offer. I accepted the inevitable consequences of the irreconcilable differences caused by my refusal to pretend, to "act as if," to "fake it 'til we make it." It was over. I already said that, didn't I? I was done. I surrendered to the tremendously fearful cultural stigma that divorce would bring down upon me, living as I did in the very heart of Utah, in the very "shadow of the everlasting hills."

Three long years of busy days and lonely nights had passed since my divorce. Now it was June, 1994. My bachelor's degree was finally in my hand. But what was I to do with it? I hadn't taken classes to prepare me to teach—the standard and most practical use of an English degree. I hadn't felt right about following that track. Believe me, after spending twenty-three years trying to make my marriage work, never feeling safe or happy, I wasn't willing to "settle" again for something I didn't want. Whatever I did for the rest of my life, I promised myself I would do it with honesty, or not at all.

In the days following my commencement, I spent hours of prayerful deliberation and meditation using my journal as a catalyst and channel of communion with my deepest inner truths. I used meditative writing—as I've since learned to call it—to explore every option I could ponder my way through. The only option that felt good to me—that burned in my bosom, that brought tears of hope and desire to my eyes—was to apply to go on in school and obtain a masters degree in English. Several of my professors encouraged me to apply; they were glad to write letters of recommendation for me. But wouldn't that just be more "impractical" training? What could I "do" with a masters degree in English? The perennial question was back, and of course it really meant, "What kind of job can you get with it?" I had no idea. Teach at a junior college? Become an editor? Those seemed like the two most logical, financially sound possibilities.

Oh, if I had only known then, dear reader, that the Lord God was going to lead me here, to this hour, to this joyful act of sharing my heart with you—my experience, strength, and hope—in the form of a collection of personal essays, I would have been so grateful and so amazed! But in the fall of 1994, I had no idea what was to come. Like Nephi in the *Book of Mormon*, I was led, not knowing beforehand what I should do (1 Nephi 4:6).

A Voice from the Fire: The Authority of Experience includes autobiographical and memoiristic essays submitted as my master's thesis in 1996. I have also included several short expository essays, written originally for *Heartbeats*, a monthly newsletter of the Heart t' Heart organization. Oh yes, and a poem or two for good measure.

The essay, "A Ramble of My Own," was originally part of the scholarly introduction to the masters thesis collection. I was tempted to leave it out, thinking it too "academic" and "dry," but when I pray about it, it *feels good*, it feels right to leave it in. I feel impressed that some one of you might enjoy an account of how the Lord led me along from emphasis to emphasis in English studies until I finally *allowed* myself to be myself and do the thing I *love*— to write personally, honestly, heart to heart, gut to gut, and soul to soul.

The second half of the original "A Ramble of My Own" essay is at the very end of this collection, retitled "A Ramble of Your Own." Here I explore the history of the personal essay. My hope in including it is kindle a flame in your heart, dear reader; to inspire you to find and explore a voice of your own.

In conclusion of this preface may I make as explicit as possible three "Articles of Belief" that stand supreme and unwavering in my soul—no matter how foolish and confusing my own choices or those of any other person in my life's story may be:

First, I believe in Christ as the Divine Son of God who lived in mortality, died, and was resurrected, *physically* and spiritually. I believe He now reigns with our Heavenly Father and communicates, as one with our Father, to our hearts and minds through the power of the Holy Ghost. I am Christian through and through and have been since my earliest recollections. Nevertheless, I honor and appreciate teachings by any organized or unorganized religious effort that encourage people to do good and love God. I trust God in the diversity of people and the spirituality of each. I believe in their right to "worship how, where, or what they may."[1] Nevertheless, the way that "works" for me is the "Way" of Christ. I worship Him and my Heavenly Father who sent Jesus to be my personal Savior and Friend.

Second, I believe in the restoration of the fullness of the original Christian theology (knowledge of God) as it is represented in the revelations of Joseph Smith, Jr. I honor him as a Prophet of God, as I honor all of the subsequent prophets and apostles who have led The Church of Jesus Christ of Latter-day Saints even to this day. I find the *theology* of Mormonism the richest, deepest, most soul satisfying rendition of Christianity that could ever be imagined by the human heart. "As man is, God once was. As God is, man may become"[2] is the core tenet of Mormon theology. No more gracious definition of mankind in relation to God has ever been offered to humanity.

Joseph Smith put it this way:

> God was once as we are now, and is an exalted man, and sits enthroned in yonder heavens! That is the great secret. If the veil were rent today, and the great God who holds this world in its orbit, and who upholds all worlds and all things by his power, was to make himself visible,—I say, if you were to see him today, you would see him like a man in form—like yourselves in all the person, image, and very form as a man... Here, then, is eternal life—to know the only wise and true God; and you have got to learn how to be Gods yourselves, and to be kings [queens] and priests [priest-esses] to God, the same as all Gods have done before you, namely, by going from one small degree to another, and from a small capacity to a great one...

> It is the first principle of the Gospel to know for a certainty the Character of God, and to know that we may converse with him as one man converses with another. (*Teachings of the Prophet Joseph Smith*, pp. 345-346, Deseret Book Company, 1974.)

This theology is my ideology, my life-blood intellectually, as well as emotionally and spiritually. Its culture is my chosen religious community and practice, despite the human foibles and failings of its members, myself included. I am, as I am prone to say, a "tee-totalin', card-carrying" member, despite injustices suffered at the hands of fellow mortal members.

In sweet conversation filled with counsel and comfort abounding, I have perceived the Lord's own words come into my mind. These words have been plainer, wiser, calmer, kinder, surer, truer than any words my often terrified, tumultuous mind could conceive or contrive. I share with you in these essays, snapshots in words—glimpses into the reality of one woman—so unique, yet so common. So strong, yet so weak. I pray you may be blessed by these moments of reflection and insight. I pray you may want to start recording your own. The whole truth is healing. It is the highest truth, the best truth, the *compound* truth that gives life and brings us to our truest potential. I bear this testimony, unceasingly, in the name of Jesus Christ, Amen.

—Colleen H.

¹*The Pearl of Great Price,* The Articles of Faith:11.

²James E. Talmage, *The Articles of Faith.* (The Church of Jesus Christ of Latter-day Saints, 1968), 430. This idea is also referenced in the following couplet from the poem "Man's Destiny" by Lorenzo Snow: "As man now is, our God once was; As now God is, so man may be,–" *Improvement Era,* 22:660-661, June 1919; also *Biography and Family Record of Lorenzo Snow,* Eliza R. Snow (Salt Lake City, 1884); *The Teachings of Lorenzo Snow,* comp. Clyde J. Williams (Salt Lake: Bookcraft, 1984), 2.

A Ramble of My Own

And I was led by the Spirit, not knowing beforehand the things which I should do. (1 Nephi 4:6)

The essayist, unlike the novelist, the poet, and the playwright, must be content in his self-imposed role of second class citizen. A writer who has his sights trained on the Nobel Prize or other earthly triumphs had best write a novel, a poem, or a play, and leave the essayist to ramble about, content with living a free life and enjoying the satisfactions of a somewhat undisciplined existence. –E.B. White[1]

J came into my English master's program in 1994, already a personal essayist by nature, living more than a "somewhat undisciplined existence." I have to admit, though, my "rambling" through life has often felt more like stumbling. I mean, I literally stumbled into writing this collection of essays, originally disguised as a scholarly thesis.

In the spirit of the true essayist, I had no clue where I was going when I started my program. It was a ramble, a "walkabout"[2] in the field of English studies, which to this day remains a cherished diversion. And even today, nearly a decade after my successful thesis defense and graduation, after years of preparation for a doctorate degree in human development and family life, I still see no closure on my "career" as an essayist. I'm not sure closure is part of an essayist's psychic paradigm.

I spent my first semester as a graduate student on familiar turf, right in the same department—the same building, the same faculty and a few of the same fellow students—as I spent the previous three years. I'm afraid I didn't feel secure or "arrived," as you'd think a person might. Instead, I felt utterly and thoroughly confused. What was I doing in classes, I kept thinking, when I should be in a therapist's office trying to survive and sort out my life? During the five years it took me to finish my bachelors work, I staggered, rather than stumbled, to school day after day. I lived through burying my oldest daughter, who died in an automobile accident so infamous I still have new acquaintances who recall hearing about it on the 10 o'clock news, over ten years ago. And then there was the ten-minute divorce proceeding that culminated twenty years of a marriage I had invested my soul in, planning on eternity.

Through the mental and emotional fog of this cumulative trauma, I vaguely understood I was expected to "declare an emphasis" for my M.A. program. I sat in my advisor's office, staring out the window as he talked to someone on the phone.

Declare an emphasis? *Emphasis: force or intensity of expression that gives importance to something.* How was I supposed to know what was important anymore? I once thought, believed, *lived* the one expression that gave my life importance—homemaking. And now I had to get a *real* education and a *real* job. Too bad I couldn't use any of the former emphases—the ones I knew so well: husband, children, diapers, menus, bottled fruit, home-made bread, handmade clothes. I didn't say any of this aloud to my advisor, of course. He finished his phone call and turned back to me. I smiled, hoping not to appear as dazed as I felt. I know how to be insane behind "just fine" smiles.

So what would my emphasis be for my graduate studies in English? What were my choices? Early British Lit, Late British Lit, Early or Late American Lit, Rhetoric, or Creative Writing. I chose "Early British Literature" for no good reason other than it was first on the list and I vaguely remembered enjoying Shakespeare, iambic pentameter, and the King James Edition of the Bible in a couple of undergraduate classes.

By the beginning of my second semester, I realized I was more fascinated with the "psychology" behind the use of language than with any literary era or style. I changed my emphasis to Rhetoric. *Rhetoric: the art of speaking or writing effectively, to persuade.*

In rhetoric classes, though, I still could not feel satisfied or settled. I found myself far too self-reflective and subjective to be a detached intellectual. While others around me were budding and blossoming into master scholars, I found myself producing pages of single-spaced personal reflections and reactions to as little as one sentence from the authors and texts we studied. I was embarrassed by my "egotism," and tried hard to be a true academic—aloof and intellectual. Most of the time, I despaired my attempts and knew they were in vain. I could not focus more than minimal attention on class assignments. My devastated psyche, staggering from the trauma I was trying to ignore, had an "assignment" I could not avoid—*comprehend your journey or die.* I spent hours writing in my personal journals. I felt like no one could teach me what I needed to know. The lessons I needed would not be found in the writings of other people.

It was nearly two years before I stumbled onto Samuel Johnson's explanation for my dilemma:

> The essayist...seldom harasses [her] reason with long
> trains of consequences, dims [her] eye with the perusal

of antiquated volumes, or burthens [her] memory with great accumulations of preparatory knowledge.[3]

Caught in this still unconscious need for self-expression, I found that no matter how hard I tried to keep my reflections and opinions to myself, I kept speaking up in class, sharing *my* thoughts on *any* and *every* subject we discussed in class.

"Could you reference that to one of the authors you were supposed to have read over the previous week?" I was asked. My teacher wanted to know I was studying.

No. These were "just" my own reflections. I had no idea, then, that I was, according to Mikhail Bakhtin's words, quoted by Peter Elbow, just coming to myself:

One's own discourse and one's own voice, although born of another or dynamically stimulated by another, will sooner or later begin to liberate themselves from the authority of the other's discourse.[4]

Meanwhile, I thought I was failing, bumping and blundering through my classes. Now, I realize I was actually being led along, all the while gaining the greatest education I could ever hope to obtain. I was coming to know *me*—my mind, my heart, my opinions—an accomplishment that, at forty-eight, was long overdue. I take solace in the promise of Christ's parable of the laborers coming to the vineyard being equally rewarded, whether they came early or late. I had to trust that getting to know me and my own "I-am" could somehow be transformed by the Lord into a masters thesis and a degree.

Still, I was not "applying" myself to gaining knowledge that I, as a single parent receiving minimal child support from my ex-husband, could use to support myself and my five minor children. How could I justify learning about something as "tangential to the marketplace"[5] as myself? I had to be *practical*. I had to prepare myself to earn a living. *Still,* I couldn't ignore the greater truth my "education" was revealing to me: "a living" wasn't something I needed to earn but something I needed to *be*; that "living" was meant to be a verb, not a noun. But where in the "discipline" of English studies could I find an environment conducive to such self-expression?

When I took my first creative writing class, it was as an elective, a fluke, another stumble. Early British Lit held nothing for me; rhetoric required burying yourself in other people's opinions, persuasions. Creative writing seemed like an easy way out of all that. After all, I had written some "creative" stuff back in Junior High. I'd even won a "creative" writing contest or two over the years.

I had to ask for special permission from my professor, Leslie Norris, since I hadn't taken any undergraduate creative writing courses. Luckily he had been my instructor in a previous class on the Romantic period in England and watched me come to tears in class over the poetry of Blake, Wordsworth, and Coleridge. He'd also worked with me directly in preparing a paper on John Donne for an undergraduate literature conference. I think he knew how desperate I was to find a place where the only endnote I needed for my work was my own byline.

As the first half of that semester passed, I sat through the other students' readings of their poetry, short stories, chapters from budding novels, and screenplays. I was awed by the collective talent around me and began to feel more and more like I had stumbled into another land where I was destined to remain a stranger, a beggar, an "also-ran." I could not produce thoughts as crystalline and succinct as the poets, though I thrilled to the freedom they took in their "associative leaps"[6] of metaphor and insight. Neither could I identify with fiction. My own experience and my own authority cried out to be acknowledged and shared, not veiled in someone else's name or character.

Gradually, amidst the confusion, I felt myself developing a definite sense of "vocation," though not in the modern, materialistic sense. No, this vocation was the kind I had read about in Scott Peck's *A World Waiting to Be Born*:

> The word vocation literally means "calling"...which may or may not coincide with one's occupation, with what one is actually doing.
>
> In this sense vocation implies a relationship. For if someone is called, something must be doing the calling...so also may some [people] spend years—even a lifetime—fleeing their true vocation...in either some kind of fear of failure or fear of success or both... So God's unique vocation for each of us invariably calls us to personal success, but not necessarily success in the world's stereotypical terms or means of measurement.[7]

It was not until midterm interviews, one-on-one, that I confessed my dilemma to Professor Norris. Haltingly I admitted to him what I am sure his sense of "vocation" as a gifted teacher had already told him—that the two poems and the several attempts at fiction I had handed in so far were *not* my forte. In one sentence he branded me and set me free: "You're a personal essayist." My lack of comprehension was thick in the air of his little office, but he only smiled warmly and continued, "Which doesn't surprise me. The personal essay is *the* genre of Mormonism because of its investment in subjective, personal experience. Subjective, highly personal experience is the very heart of your religion, you know?"

No, I didn't know that. I thought losing yourself to serve others was the very heart of my religion.

The rest of the semester went more smoothly for me as I reworked a couple of essays I had written several years before, borrowing the style of the late Erma Bombeck. I still wasn't brave enough to let go and create brand new material from my current life experience. I wasn't sure how to write about the drastic turn my life had taken in recent years. Besides, who in the LDS culture would want to read of such imperfection and uncertainty?

The next semester I took a second creative writing course, determined to hold my own in the midst of the poets and short story writers. I still wasn't sure I belonged, but I was sure I wanted to be there. Then God arranged what Scott Peck calls a "graceful intervention,"[8] which set my feet squarely on the path of the personal essayist.

Phillip Lopate, author of a highly acclaimed and definitive work on the personal essay, *The Art of the Personal Essay*, came to Brigham Young University and to my 518R class. Enthralled, I followed him from my class to another class and to his afternoon reading. I would have followed him home if I'd had the airfare. Instead I invested in his book. As I read, I wept with relief to find permission to own my own style—vernacular, conversational, intimately honest; my own genre—personal, self-revelatory, rambling, tentative, not complete: in other words—my own voice. By the end of that semester I knew where I belonged, where I was called. For better or worse, I filled out the paperwork to change my emphasis one last time.

[1] E.B. White, *Essays of E.B. White*. (New York: Harper & Row, 1979); quoted in Phillip Lopate, *The Art of the Personal Essay: An Anthology from the Classical Era to the Present*. (New York: Doubleday, 1994), xxxiii.

[2] Phillip Lopate, *The Art of the Personal Essay: An Anthology from the Classical Era to the Present*. (New York: Doubleday, 1994), xli.

[3] Samuel Johnson, The Rambler, p. 201; quoted in Carl Klaus, "Essayists on the Essay," in *Literary Nonfiction: Theory, Criticism, Pedagogy*, ed. Chris Anderson (Carbondale: Southern Illinois UP), 158.

[4] Peter Elbow, "The Pleasures of Voice," *Literary Nonfiction: Theory, Criticism, Pedagogy*, ed. Chris Anderson (Carbondale: Southern Illinois UP), 230.

[5] Lopate, xxxiii.

[6] Phillip Lopate, "An Interview with Phillip Lopate," interview by John Bennion, *AWP Chronicle*, no. 4, vol. 28 (February 1996): 1.

[7] M. Scott Peck, *A World Waiting to Be Born: Civility Rediscovered*, (New York: Bantam, 1993), 61-63, 67.

[8] Ibid., 77.

Words

Dear God!
I am filled with such fire,
Such burning,
Such energy!
How stilted,
How black and white
These words look.
There's no way
To catch the fire,
No way to say the
Burning.
And in the trying
The energy is thinned.
Thinned to words.
Mere words.
But words are
All
I have.
Words will have to do.
Words that only mumble,
Barely whisper
What I hear
In stereophonic sound,
Standing in the midst
Of the choir,
Singing my heart out.

A Voice from the Fire

*When writing about real life, I never cease to struggle
with the problem of where to begin and where to end.
This dilemma does as much to convince me of life's
infinite nature as any religious dogma.*

—C. C. Harrison

The other day I lamented to a close friend, "Trying to
find the time in my life to write is like being a war corre-
spondent writing under fire—with bombs falling everywhere." She
entirely missed my play for sympathy. She laughed instead and
replied, "Remember—that's how the 'Star Spangled Banner' was
written."

Writing under fire. I muse on the words.

My heart was hot within me, while I was musing the fire burned. (Psalms 39:3)

I wonder if writing under fire could be compared to trying to breathe under water. It's hard not to get some of it down your throat and need to cough it up when you surface.

I will make my words in thy mouth fire. (Jeremiah 5:14)

Once a fire begins it doesn't ask permission or offer an apology for the shape and size it takes. Give it an inch and it'll take a mile. Give it a twig and it'll take the forest. And all that fire begins with just a little smoke in tender places.

I love to sit and watch the flames in a fireplace or campfire. Here they shimmer along the edge of a log, a line of light barely above its surface. In another place they leap and fall back. Big, little. Here, there. Bursting into existence out of thin air, then disappearing in an instant. Under these circumstances, flames are so warm. So comforting. So fascinating. So harnessed.

Watching this fearsome power stay tenuously within bounds is mesmerizing. And when the flame's dance of leaping, licking energy overwhelms my senses, I stare instead into the white hot space at the center of the crisscrossed logs where the tinder first began to smoke. The coals there glow as if they are alive with a glory that has purged them of all physical substance. Still, they keep their form. They are the last to know they're being consumed—transformed into pure energy. Reduced to ashes.

Annie Dillard once wrote, "When you write, you lay out a line of words. The line of words is a miner's pick, a wood-carver's gouge, a surgeon's probe. You wield it, and it digs a path you follow."[1] I'd like to offer from my experience one more metaphor for this "line of words" that picks, gouges, and probes. It is a line of fire that I cannot avoid, no matter how hard I try. It penetrates my heart.

Fire changes things. Absolutely, molecularly.

Writing under fire does the same thing.

$\wp$

And now when the flames began to scorch him, he cried unto them... (Mosiah 17:14)

I'm coming to realize that victimization and martyrdom have only one distinguishing difference: a martyr is a victim with a message; a victim is a martyr without a voice.

From an eternal perspective, there is no tragedy in martyrdom. It represents the unfolding of a preordained destiny. In the process of fulfilling that destiny, the martyr finds herself blessed with a foretaste of exaltation as she discovers she is not alone in her suffering.

My God hath sent his angel, and hath shut the lions' mouths, that they have not hurt me. (Daniel 6:22)

She also discovers God has no fear of fire.

He answered and said, Lo, I see four men loose, walking in the midst of the fire,... the fourth is like the Son of God. (Daniel 3:25)

In contrast, the tragedy of victimization is the sacrifice is secret, silent, wasted. The victim, overwhelmed by the lies of her adversary—her perpetrator—suffers the soul-searing fires of shame and guilt, and dies without protest. The forces of evil are left unimpeded; they go on to destroy other innocents.

I know what it means to be a victim. I learned very early to suffer silently, to be terrified of drawing fire.

My parents drank a lot, and when they drank they fought, physically as well as verbally. Sometimes their fights went on for hours. I often hid alone in a closet, waiting for their rage to decide my future—whether I could eventually come out of hiding and sneak back into my own bed to suck my thumb and clutch the pillow I couldn't sleep without—or whether one of them would kill the other.

I was only five, but I'd seen dead things. Dead animals on the road, dead chickens my father butchered, dead dogs he shot. What if? What if one of these nights while he's fighting with my mother he gets as mad at her as he did at those dogs last summer. I can still hear the shotgun blast. I can still see the blood.

The dogs were fighting when my dad drove up in his pickup. He was late coming home from work; probably stopped off for a few beers. My mom was screaming at the dogs and squirting them with a garden hose. Neither dog cared for anything except killing the other. They were bitter enemies, far more than instinct called for. "Highball" had been my parent's pet since before I was born. I didn't know life without him. He was big and black and had the nature of a saint. At least until Danny came. Danny was a purebred English pointer my father had purchased for only one reason—to breed to Pepper, the purebred bitch we'd raised from a puppy. Highball was jealous. He had a murderous hatred of Danny. Nothing would deter him from the chance that came to him when he escaped his dog run that afternoon and found Danny was also free.

Shouting and swearing at me and my mother as much as at the dogs, my father came out of his truck, running, shotgun in hand. It was duck and pheasant season in California, and he was never unprepared for hunting. My mother backed away from the dogs— or maybe from the gun.

At that moment Danny broke Highball's death grip and took off running across our half-acre backyard. My dad followed the dogs, still shouting. He screamed at me to shut the gate so they couldn't get through into the side yard and the grape orchard beyond. I didn't get to the gate in time. Danny was there before me, Highball literally on his tail.

Shoving me aside, my father went through the gate after them. Just past the fence made of chicken wire, Highball caught Danny and began to maul him again. I stood and watched as my dad lifted his gun and took aim. He hesitated, waiting for the dogs to separate. He was willing to kill Highball in an attempt to save Danny's expensive bloodlines. Just then Danny bolted from under Highball's jaws. The sound of the gun reverberated off the fence, the house, the trees, the garage and back again.

Highball dropped without a sound. Danny only stumbled and then kept running—right for me. There was blood along his side where the birdshot had peppered him.

In terror I turned and fled up the back steps of my house. I inadvertently flung the screen door wide open, giving Danny time to come in behind me. In his death throes, running on instinct alone, he followed me as I ran through the kitchen, the dining room, the living room and out the screen door to the front yard. He left a trail of blood all the way. Finally, in the front flower bed, amidst my mother's favorite pansies, he dropped dead. I collapsed behind a tree in our front yard and sobbed. Later I watched my mother scrub the blood out of the carpet and water it into the pansies' roots.

What if during one of their fights I came out of the closet when the silence fell and found blood everywhere? My mother's blood. Or my father's.

That very next winter, I stood alongside my mother by the kitchen stove; my mother dressed only in her underwear and a blanket. She had stripped off her wet, muddy clothes on the back porch. Mud dripped from her hair and from under the blanket. My eyes just cleared the top of the stove. I watched the burners turn red-hot for warmth. The oven was cracked open for the same reason. My mother was shivering. Though it seldom snows in the Sacramento valley, the winter rain can be near freezing. My dad had thrown her in a mud hole in the grape orchard next to our house, then taken off in his truck.

I looked up into my mother's face; it was swollen with tears and with drink. She had a butcher knife in her hand. "I'm going to kill that b—," she hissed, "the next time he steps through that door." She opened another can of beer and sat down at the kitchen table to wait. I slipped away to the bathroom to wipe the muddy water off my feet. Back in bed I fell asleep, waiting for my father to come home, hoping he wouldn't, wishing him dead, just not at my mother's hand.

When I'm "writing down the bones"[2] like this, as Natalie Goldberg puts it—facing the truth about my life, either past or present—it feels like I'm scraping bone and finding fire.

But his word was in mine heart as a burning fire shut up in my bones, and I was weary with forbearing, and I could not stay. (Jeremiah 20:9)

I can't write the truth in my life without feeling the fire of it. And feeling the fire, I can hardly write. But I have to. I have to tell someone about this life I've lived and am still living. It's important for me—and maybe for others. The imperative to do so burns in me with all the fire of God's own truth—plainly I cannot deny it. I can't be silent any longer.

$$\mathcal{S}$$

Like a novice behind convent walls, I spent most of my life cloistering my writing away within the pages of my journals, barely whispering lest I disturb anyone. As a child I made up poems and stories as I played with the written word, rejoicing in its inherent silence. As an adult, I filled my journal with the litany and rituals of a dedicated Mormon woman's service to husband, children, home, church, and community all in the name of serving God (Mosiah 2:17). I had no idea at the time that, as the "good son" in the story of the prodigal[3] so poignantly demonstrates, serving someone is not always the equivalent of knowing them. You can serve someone for a lifetime and never come to know them.

Then came the day when I finally realized how little I knew God or those I served. The god I made of the successful family was ripped away from me by another's agency. All my efforts to keep up a facade of "fineness," while silently absorbing and denying twenty-three years of continuous abuse, were destroyed in the flaming light of truth.

The first truth that could not be disguised or ignored, whitewashed or driven into hiding, was that my oldest daughter, Karen, always the much-loved overachiever, was dropping out of our "fine" looking Mormon world and into the world of drug use. First, Vivarin, then cigarettes, then alcohol, then marijuana—the progression taking only weeks—driven on by my hysterical attempts to reason with her.

In the middle of one particularly virulent argument with her, she shredded my mind with the second truth—the truth her plunge into self-destruction was masking. She had been sexually abused, repeatedly, and by someone close, trusted. Someone she had known all her life. She had tried to keep it to herself. Tried to pretend it didn't matter. Tried to pretend that being very, very active in church and school would drown out the shame of it, but she couldn't stand it anymore. I was shocked beyond belief. I had heard stories like this in the recovery groups I attended. I had come to believe deeply that most sin—even a sin as perverse as victimizing a child—was the action of an addict, someone who had gradually lost the ability to resist by repeated and ever-worsening indulgences. I knew what it felt like to be so stripped of dignity, of worth, of choice. I was a recovering food addict at this point in my life, thanks to the power of God as I best understood Him. Addiction had taken its toll in so many ways in our family, generation after generation—and now this most tragic intrusion of its ugly reality! This was enough. We had to come out of denial and secrecy, and this was the place to begin.

Gradually, Karen stopped sobbing. I reassured her she'd be able to put the burden down now. Did she know this wasn't her fault? That she had been (was still) only a child? That she wasn't to blame? Finally she was able to dry her face. She noticed the time. She had to be to work in a few minutes. I asked her if she'd be willing to talk to "the authorities" about this. Her face filled with such terror, I was terrified for her. No. No. She couldn't talk to anyone—especially to a man. No one would believe her. No one would take her seriously. They would blame her. She almost raved these things as the tears began to spill again. She put her hands over her face and sobbed with the depth of her beliefs. I cringed before the heart-rending energy of her surety. Where had she learned to expect such negation of her self, of her words, her truth? I knew, but I recoiled from knowing.

As the afternoon passed and my younger daughters came home from school, I privately talked with each one of them. Two of them admitted to similar experiences with this same individual. Shortly after, my husband arrived home. I asked if we could have a private talk. I usually tried to give him plenty of space when he first came into the house. He was often surly, sometimes brutal if approached too abruptly. On this particular day, however, I was past the point of fearing his wrath. In the privacy of our bedroom, I poured out the girls' stories to him. I could tell by the expression on his face that these shameful circumstances were going to be minimized, rationalized, and left to fester—just as we had always minimized our own secret addictions. No, no, I pled with him. We can't keep pretending everything's fine in our lives! We've got to face the truth about covert addiction and its devastation in our squeaky clean Mormon culture. This wasn't a little, "socially acceptable" behavior, like overeating or overworking! We couldn't keep the lid on this. It was terrible to admit and to face now, but if we didn't, it could destroy our daughters' lives and enable and allow our community to grow sicker. We had to go straight to the bishop with this.

My husband disagreed. It wasn't that bad. We could take care of it within the family. It would make nothing but trouble for everyone. And what if they were just making it up. What if it was an excuse Karen was using as a diversion from the real truth—that she was a wayward, unrighteous child? This was all a big overre-action on my part, what with all my crazy friends claiming to have been abused as children. We should let it go. If I made a big deal out of this, everyone in the family would have hell to pay for it. The members of our ward would withdraw from us. We'd be branded and labeled in our entire social circle. What was I thinking? I must be insane!

For once I was not willing to go along with my husband's opinion, no matter how scornfully and bitterly he painted the picture of the consequences. I prayed about my daughters' stories. I knew by a witness to my heart, burning inside me like a tremen-dous flame—they were *not* lying. I insisted we immediately make an appointment to meet with the bishop of our ward. My husband would not come with me. Our girls, who had overheard our raised voices and his angry denouncement of their story and pronouncement of my gullibility, also refused to go with me. With sobbing anger, they attacked me. What was I trying to do by going to the bishop? Make a spectacle of us all?

Still, I *had* to come out of hiding. I had to let someone know what was happening in our home. I couldn't bear to have another layer of secret shame riveted onto my children's hearts. I called our bishop's executive secretary and made an appointment for that evening.

I recounted my daughters' stories to my bishop, beginning with Karen's. He knew her as a feisty, smart-aleck, recently turned wild, teenager; I couldn't meet his eyes. What if I didn't see respect and belief there? Without pausing I plunged ahead into my other girls' accounts. I felt like I was throwing up raw sewage. When I finally looked up, my bishop was visibly shaken by my tearful account. He couldn't understand why I was alone, though. Why hadn't my husband come with me? And where were my daughters? He wanted to talk to each of them, personally. I told him how they reacted to my invitation to come with me—they were terrified, angry, resistant, belligerent. I was convinced by the desperate sincerity of their reactions that while it was time for me to start talking about the secret troubles in our family, it was not the right time for them. It can take years for a sexual abuse victim—or *any* kind of abuse victim for that matter—to face the truth of their degradation, much less talk openly about it.

Then why had they told me? I don't know. Maybe, it was time to *begin* telling. Maybe because they felt safe with me? Maybe because they wanted and needed someone to advocate for them?

I could tell by the expression on his face that my bishop was still perplexed by this whole irrational, twisted business of abuse and how victims try to hide what they suffer from so tragically. He couldn't understand why, if you are really being hurt, you wouldn't take the opportunity to speak up about it.

I sat in silence. I sensed there was nothing else I could say. He was already overwhelmed. After telling me he would have to report this to the State Division of Family Services and I would probably be hearing from them soon, he thanked me for coming in and rose to see me out of his office. We were already well over my standard fifteen minute allotment of time. A couple coming to renew their temple recommends waited in the hall outside his office. As he opened the door for me, a smile returned to his face as he greeted the cheerful couple. He thanked me again—with a smile—for coming in. I was grateful the bishop could end his evening of interviews on a more positive note.

Later, when the bishop called my husband in to "confirm" my story, my husband minimized and white-washed the situation even more than he had with me. He portrayed to the bishop that, speaking confidentially, the "real problem" was actually more in my overactive imagination than in reality. After all, I had been attending support group meetings for people who, like myself, struggled with compulsive eating disorders. He'd gone himself a few times, just to humor me. As far as he could tell, the people I met there spent most of their time filling each others' heads with excuses of how their childhood abuse caused addictive behaviors, including overeating. Since Karen had been acting crazy lately, starting to experiment with alcohol and drugs, and since all the younger girls were struggling with overeating, he suggested I had gotten it into my head that abuse was at the bottom of it. I had probably led the girls on with suggestive questions and then over-reacted to their responses. Women were like that, you know. Hysterical, hypersensitive—and I was one of the worst, according to him. (Please note: I wasn't privy to this exchange between my husband and my bishop. I am reporting what my husband reported to me, when he came home from the interview, smug and tri-umphant—as if he had just scored some sort of a victory over me.)

A few hours later, when my husband's usual attitude of bitter-ness returned full force, he made sure to describe how embarrassed and apologetic the bishop was for calling the State Division of

Family Services and informing Stake leaders of my report. He and the bishop agreed that one of the best ways to handle this situation was for me to stop associating with such over-reactive, self-pitying people as I met at these strange, *non-LDS* support meetings I attended. I sat in battered silence. If the blows to my mind and heart, to my spirit and psyche had been physical, I would have needed a quick trip to the nearest emergency room. But the pain wasn't over.

A few days later, a state social worker came to our home in the middle of the day. She looked around our home, which was reasonably clean. There were pictures of the temple and of Jesus on our walls, along with smiling family portraits. A *Book of Mormon* sat on the end table, the local LDS music station was playing on the radio in the kitchen, the smell of baking bread was in the air. She sat down and interviewed me. I told her my story as understated and calmly as I could. After all, I didn't want her to see me acting like the hysterical, crazy person those with authority apparently discerned me to be. By the time we were through, as insane as it sounds now, I found myself telling her my daughters' stories probably *were* just to get attention and that my oldest daughter really was a pretty "flaky" person—doing the shameful drugs and alcohol scene. For all we knew, one of her crazy addict friends could have put her up to it. In fact, maybe it was all a ploy to punish me and her father. The social worker expressed her appreciation for my candidness and went back to her office to close the case. False alarm.

I didn't attend as many support meetings as before. After all, I was starting to sound like a crazy person.

Eventually the word spread throughout the ward that Colleen was having problems, some sort of breakdown—mental, emotional, or maybe even spiritual in nature. She was making up crazy stories about her daughters being sexually abused—trying to find some excuse for her oldest girl's wild actions.

The bishop and his wife made a special visit to talk to me. I told them the truth—that I felt like I was going under, like I was drowning in my own enforced silence and other's misjudgment. Within a week I was taken out of my service position in the Young Women's organization. I was given no other calling in my ward. My days were filled with a strange, screaming silence. No phone calls. No lessons to prepare or planning meetings to attend. No assignments of any kind. It was the first time in thirty years as a member of the Church that I hadn't held at least one calling.

I staggered. I reeled. I crashed. I burned.

I couldn't understand what was happening. What about *my* testimony? What about *my* word? Didn't *my* life of faithfulness and service in the Church and community speak for my integrity and sanity? Since the day I joined the Church at the age of fourteen, I had given my life to it. For over thirty years I participated in full fellowship. I was in continuous possession of a temple recommend since my temple sealing in 1968. I had quit college to have my twelve children and to support my husband in his career. I was a graduate of the Church's seminary and Institute of Religion programs. How could anyone think I would tell such a story to my bishop if it were not true?

As the reality of my suspect and devalued position in the religious community I had cherished since my early teens settled into my heart, it compounded the pain of realizing that my husband of twenty-three years found so much satisfaction in the shame and blame I was subjected to. The fire raged within the whited sepulcher and the facade of pretense and lies began to blister and peel.

∅

Weeks passed. As the silence around me got thicker, the silence within me grew deeper. I had always been an enthusiastic journal keeper. Now, I sat and stared at my journal. I felt null, void. What would I fill its pages with, anyhow? Zeroes? Ciphers? I couldn't find a voice—not even a writing voice. It had been demonstrated to me as plainly as it could be that neither my thoughts nor my words were of any value. They were as so much drivel, nonsense, not to be taken seriously.

I could no longer pretend things were "fine," sufficient, adequate, bearable—that I was a happy, cherished, honored member of my family *or my culture*. I felt as if my life were draining out of a heart pierced with deep wounds—great gaping holes from which nothing but questions, pain, sorrow, and confusion spilled forth. Finally, my confusion got so bad that I knew I had to take up my pen again or truly suffer a complete mental breakdown—just as my husband predicted.

But how could I tell the truth about this pain? I felt the Spirit of Truth testifying to me that I could not write again until I told the *whole* truth. I couldn't white-wash and pretend to myself in my journals any longer. I had to open up and let the words that came out reveal the whole truth about my life and the circumstances I was in. Sobbing, writing in script the size of a second grader's, I began to write. It felt like I was writing in blood and tears combined as they gushed forth from my broken heart.

To tell the whole truth about my life—how I thought, felt, believed, and didn't believe—felt like hell at first. The process was so unfamiliar, so unpopular in my cultural context. Gradually, though, as I died to everything else but my own unveiled truth— the ugly as well as the pleasant—I began to develop an affinity for truth, a hunger for it. As I recoiled from the pretense and sham around me, in my home and in my culture, I instinctively turned to the words of the prophets, both ancient and modern. Here was truth, canonized. If I was going to find truth in this world, it would be through their guidance.

I knew I could trust the scriptures, particularly the *Book of Mormon*. After all, it was written and preserved especially for these last days. That book became a font of living water as I used my journal and pen to ponder my way through each verse. Between the revelations of Nephi and Benjamin, Alma and Moroni, I began to record the personal revelation that came to me as I likened their words to my own life. I began to know the Lord as I had never known Him in all my years of dutiful service. I found myself looking unto Him in more and more of my thoughts, living for the day when I would be perfected in Him and have the humility to look unto Him in *every* thought. My soul was filled with a new fire as He drew near to me in Spirit and counseled me with His own words through the Gift and power of the Holy Ghost. I found that Christ—His *living* reality, His precious words—was the true "gift of the Holy Ghost."

For I, saith the LORD, *will be unto her a wall of fire round about, and will be the glory in the midst of her. Zechariah 2:5*

I know when I am in the presence of significant truth because somewhere in "the midst" of me, a full, burning, swelling sensation begins. The hair on my body stands on end as if I've just changed temperatures. My breathing pattern changes, becoming shallower, quicker. My throat tightens up. My eyes have a sensation of pressure in them, a burning that precedes, and often becomes, tears.

Sometimes, in especially powerful and prolonged spiritual situations, this awareness of truth begins as a sensation of warmth at the crown of my head that moves down over my shoulders, rejoices in my burning heart, descends into my bowels, passes through my loins and weakens my legs. A trembling begins deep inside me, as if a quake is beginning at the hot, molten core of the earth instead of on its surface. If it continues to increase, it eventually reaches the surface of my soul, and my body begins to shake. When I am under this influence I feel something changing, breaking apart at my core. It is my heart. Within my heart I find a white-hot ember that is not consumed by the fire, but welcomes it. I feel a heaviness across my shoulders like invisible wings, like a weight of glory. My entire body feels tense—energized—poised for flight. The question always remains—will it be flight to God or away from Him? With my revealed heart filled with the everlasting burning of my own "I AM," will I come to Him or run from Him?

To Him! To Him! Lord, I will come to Thee. Follow Thee. Cleave unto Thee above all others!

I feel like I am on a high mountain. All things that are expedient for me to see or know are given me in the hour I need them. And with the eyes of my understanding I see that God is over and above and around and through all things. I no longer know it just from the prophet's testimony (D&C 88:13). I have "seen" it. I have "heard" His own testimony of it. I have experienced it. It is filed in my brain cells under "reality"—not fantasy, or even faith.

From this high place I see I am, like Nephi, "highly favored of the Lord," even though I have "seen many afflictions in all my days" (1 Nephi 1:1). He has given me His heart and His mind in return for mine. I am aware that everything that happens in this world, happens according to His allowance—even evil. There is a purpose in all things—even the challenge of evil, of victimization and martyrdom—to prove the hearts of everyone involved, both the victims and the perpetrators. There are no coincidences; no mistakes, *nothing* His Mercy and Power can not, will not, and does not satisfy and make right. There is a love so encompassing, so penetrating, so all consuming, it is the reason for our very existence. It is the source from which we came and it is our destiny as soon as we choose it. No matter how long any of us resist—though it might be forever—this love will wait. This is the love that suffereth long and is kind. It is the pure love of Christ that fuels every good life—no matter what other religious traditions have named Him. This is His love and it is mine and I am consumed in it.

Though this relationship is communicated to me as Joseph Smith once described, through "the spirit of revelation" or "pure intelligence,"[4] I record it in the "weakness of my own language" as conversations with the Lord. As miraculous as it may sound, I have found God willing to converse with me, even as Joseph promised, "as one [person] with another,"[5] and to counsel me, literally, in all my "doings"—even through the time of Karen's sudden death, four short months after her disclosure.

♌

"The Spirit of God, like a fire is burning..." I can hear the Tabernacle Choir tape plainly from my car stereo, even though the car is parked several yards away. I left the tape playing on purpose. It helps at times like this.

I sit in the early afternoon sun and watch ants scurry in and out of the shady crevices of the carving on my daughter's headstone. I begin to sweat, but sitting by Karen's grave, I find some reason to enjoy the heat. Somehow the heat is less annoying when sitting with someone who will never feel it again.

February 3, 1971 — August 26, 1989. I stare at the dates on the headstone, repeating the math over and over in my mind, wondering if it will ever make sense—if the numbers will ever stop looking like an advanced calculus formula that means absolutely *nothing* to my mortal mind. Eighteen years, six months and twenty-three days. No matter how you look at it, it doesn't add up to nearly enough birthdays.

I just celebrated my forty-eighth. I stopped that day, as I do every year, and smiled at the black mug on my bookshelf above my computer. Karen gave it to me at my fortieth birthday party, laughing and hugging me and insisting I take it *seriously*. It reads, "I'd rather be forty than pregnant." It's strange, especially with three grand-babies due in the next month, to think she'll never be either forty or pregnant. Still, something reminds me I can trust God in all things, including this. It's been seven years since her death. Five since my divorce.

Karen's plot is at the top of Orem City's cemetery, near the chainlink fence that separates the green lawns from the now dry October hillside. The hills are crisscrossed with dirt-bike and hiking trails. She loved biking and hiking and skiing and softball and dancing and...

Trust God in all things.

I brush dry grass clippings off the flat stone at her head and study another grave only fifteen feet away, decorated for the impending holiday—Halloween. A large tole-painted red wagon filled with three little children in costumes—a devil, a ghost, and a bat—is nearby several plastic jack-o-lanterns, the kind children collect candy in. I sit and wonder if there might be candy in them. Parents do strange and tender things when their children precede them in death.

I get on my knees, crawl over to Karen's side of the stone and lie out flat on the grass, on my back, my face to the sky. It's a "thing" I do occasionally—lying on her grave—sort of an exercise in going down into the *depths* of humility.

In the seven years since that hot August afternoon when she and some friends filled "Big Gulp" cups with a little Coke and a lot of rum and took off for Lagoon to meet some guys—and never made it; since that hour when she went through her friend's wind-shield head first and ended up on the other side of the sky in some other time and space, I haven't come here as often as a dutiful mother should, but I've come as often as my heart could bear it.

I've missed most of the anniversaries of her birthday and her death-day. I especially avoid public days of remembrance—Memorial Day, holidays. I didn't come up on that first Christmas.

Throughout the traditional Christmas activities that first year after her death, we all pretended to be "okay" without her, mentioning her only now and then, joking about her sense of humor. She would have wanted it that way.

Our reenactment of the birth of Christ—replete with improvised costumes for Herod and his soldiers as well as the wise men, shepherds, angels, donkey, and sheep—left me crying. Even though we went high-tech and rigged up a shop light on a pole so our angel could stand on the piano bench and hold it over the stable scene, I kept "seeing" another angel—a skinny little girl with wispy blond hair feathered out from her head—reacting to the static electricity in the tinsel halo she wore. I remembered the snapshot taken when ten-year-old Karen played the angel, standing on the piano bench draped in a white sheet, wearing tinsel garland around her head and holding a big aluminum foil-covered cardboard star out over the "manger" (a cardboard box) where her own favorite doll lay. All the other children, dressed as the holy couple, the shepherds, wise men, or sheep, knelt in adoration. Remembering her as that angel put the idea in my head: I had to go out to the cemetery and lie down on her grave as soon as we had our first heavy snowfall.

The snow finally came. For a night and two days it fell almost continuously. Late on the second evening it slowed and then stopped. I waited until after dinner and dishes were finished to leave the house. No one noticed me leaving and I didn't expect to be gone long. I wanted to go alone so I didn't tell anyone. It was only a three-minute drive and I was pretty sure no one else would be there on such a night.

After negotiating the unplowed lanes of the cemetery, I parked my car under a street light near her grave. I sat in my car for a long time, contemplating the stretch of virgin snow between me and the little tree next to Karen's grave. I didn't want anyone to see what I was about to do and think I was crazy. I wasn't trying to be crazy. I was trying to be honest—honest about how much I missed her; how much I longed to be close to her physically—just one last time. After all, her physical self was the part I had been God's instrument in giving her. I ached to hold her in my arms once more.

Mustering the courage to get out of the car and wade through the snow, I lay down on her grave that night, ignoring the cold creeping through my jacket. I fantasized about what I *wished* the police and paramedics had said to me that August afternoon. "Mrs. Bowman, your daughter has made a terrible mess up here on I-15. We're going to need you to come clean up after her and take her home." I would have. I would have gone and gathered what was left of her in my arms and held her on that drive to Holy Cross Hospital. I would have been as blessed to be covered with her blood then as she had been to be covered with mine eighteen years before on the night of her birth.

Lying in the snow in the cemetery that night, trying to grasp the fact that my child was dead *before* me—such an out-of-space, out-of-time, out-of-sync, out-of-whack, out-of-my-mind sort of thought—was the coldest I've ever been in my life.

Cold or not, I couldn't stand up until I fulfilled my original intention, a singularly irrational urge—to make the biggest snow angel I could right there on her grave. Spreading my arms over and over again, I tried to create wings worthy of her. I had never made a snow angel in my life, though it had been her favorite winter thing to do. Exhausted from pushing the snow back and forth, I stopped and watched the steam from my breath rise into the black night sky and smiled at the joy I felt. In my mind's eye I could see her flashing smile. I wondered just how far God allowed proxy work to go.

"*Mom! Mom! Watch me! Watch this!*" *She waved to me from the front lawn of our family home in north Orem. Her friends stood watching her from the street. Some of them had already piled into the Blazer. A couple were securing her skis to the ski rack on top of the car. The exhaust from the tailpipe and the breath from all their faces rose into the air. The sky was bright blue. Twenty-seven degrees under clear skies. Eight inches of new snow in the valleys. Twenty-four new at Snowbird on a base of eighty-four inches. Karen was a snow-bunny of the highest rank. She had been one ever since she saw her first snowstorm—a freak event in Las Vegas back in '73. She had been two.*

Now, with only a week until her eighteenth birthday, and a day of skiing ahead of her, she glowed so bright I thought her entire form would melt into the flat, untouched expanse on our lawn as she prepared to fall straight backwards into the snow. Holding her arms out at right angles to her body, she smiled up at me to make sure I was still watching. I was the exact opposite of Karen in my absolute abhorrence of cold and snow. I clutched the top of my house-robe around me and let the hot air from the vent at my feet balloon out the skirt of my nightgown. I raised one arm, waved, and smiled back. Our eyes met and a hint of the old energy sparkled, the love energy that passed so freely between us when she was younger.

Why was it that in these last few years the farther apart we were the more we could relax and connect? Just typical teenage with-drawal from parents was what I wanted to believe, but some part of me knew better. Somewhere inside me I could sense a despair in her distant expressions, in her eyes. Sometimes, when our eyes met, I'd feel like a peasant woman in the middle ages watching my child carried off over the shoulder of an enemy warrior as part of the plunder from our village. But having just been beaten into submission and raped myself, I could do nothing but sit by my burning house and watch her disappear.

I tried not to let tears well up as I waved to her from the window. She fell back into the snow in slow motion, yelling out a war-whoop as she fell. All her friends roared with laughter and called out her name. Their voices rang through the otherwise pristine Sabbath silence of our ninety-five percent Mormon neighborhood. I tried not to think of the fact that these kids were taking more than skis to the slopes with them; somewhere in all their preparations, they had made sure to procure enough pot and booze to make the day really fly.

After opening and closing her legs and lifting and closing her arms several times to make the angel, Karen jumped to her feet, squealing with delight. She stood on the sidewalk, triumphant, while a couple of friends helped her brush the fresh powder from her snowbibs, her jacket, and her ski cap. Then one by one they squeezed into the car. I'm sure there were not enough seat belts for them all. Karen was the last one in. Just before pulling the door closed behind her she turned and gave me a thumbs up. I waved feebly and dropped my arm to my side.

I thought of the snowy roads up Provo Canyon, the icy river that ran below the road, the sharp turns. I thought of the lack of adequate seat belts. Even the kids who had them probably weren't wearing them. These were young people who, though raised in families where law and order was preached, seemed to have no inclination to respect it.

After they were gone I stood for a few moments and looked at the snow angel on the front lawn. No reason to hold back the tears then.

Or now.

As a woman—the traditional victim figure, along with children—I have only one power and that is to "cry out." And I see by the scriptures that this crying out is actually very powerful when we cry out to God.

And the sobbings of their hearts ascend up to God against you. (Jacob 2:35)

While it is true that I have no truth and no voice that God doesn't give me, it is not true that God gives me no voice or no truth.

He has given me *this* voice—this mind, these feelings, this life. Through the crucible of this life, I have come to know several truths that His testimony has confirmed to my heart with an undeniable burning.

Did not our heart burn within us, while he talked with us by the way, and while he opened to us the scriptures? (Luke 24:32)

Life has taught me a few truths that Christ's own testimony to my heart and mind has confirmed. By His testimony, administered to me by the power and Gift of the Holy Ghost, I know these things are true:

The Church of Jesus Christ of Latter-day Saints is all it claims to be. It is true even when the people aren't.

"The priesthood" is not the *men* in the Church, though we often use the word to imply that. We say things like, "My husband is the priesthood in our home." "The priesthood will be meeting at 9:00 A.M., next Sunday." The priesthood is the authority to act in the name of God, and some men honor that authority and administer it humbly and prayerfully. Others do not understand the solemn obligation that goes with such authority—the obligation to live and behave as nearly like the Lord Jesus Christ and their Heavenly Father as they humanly can (D&C 121:39).

Power in the priesthood is not an exact synonym for offices, keys, or even for patriarchy. Power in the priesthood is synonymous with Christ, who lives just beyond the veil of mortality and assures me that His power is upon me and upon my children, regardless of the actions or opinions of any man—including their father.

There is *one* family that most certainly is forever and can be counted on, no matter what happens in mortality. That family unit is the Eternal Family of God. "I am a daughter of a Heavenly Father who loves me…" *That* is forever. My two grandchildren, born out of wedlock and adopted and sealed to other parents and grandparents, are *still* in *my* Eternal Family. According to their faithfulness and mine, we will enjoy each other's company and love some day.

Despite a popular prophetic misquote to the contrary, I have found there is *one* success that *can* compensate for failure in the home—in fact it compensates, amends, and heals *every* failure eventually. It is to come to know the pure love of Christ. It is to come to love the fire ignited by the Word of the Lord to your soul.

A victim is a martyr without a voice. A martyr is a victim that has found her voice. Exquisite pain becomes exquisite joy when Truth is loved and spoken in plainness and humility. It is my prayer that the only Muse[6] I trust, even the Spirit of Truth,[7] will possess me in this work, be with me in the fire, and transform the fires of martyrdom for both me and my children into the fires of exaltation.

For this purpose I cry from the fire.

[1]Annie Dillard, *The Writing Life,* (New York: Harper and Rowe, 1989), 3.

[2]Natalie Goldberg, *Writing Down the Bones: Freeing the Writer Within,* (Boston: Shambala, 1986).

[3]Luke 15:11–32

[4]Joseph Smith, *Teachings of the Prophet Joseph Smith*, ed. Joseph Fielding Smith (Salt Lake City: Deseret, 1974), 151.

[5]Ibid., 345.

[6] "A source of inspiration, especially a guiding genius." *Merriam Webster Collegiate Dictionary, Tenth Edition.*

[7] *Doctrine and Covenants* 88:66; 93:8–9; 103:20.

Conversion

My God,
There is before me an altar,
Invisible to the eye
As are
My offerings,
Invisible.
My life,
My will,
My heart—
All of me, uncreated
And sovereign
Self,
I place there.
A mixture of both good
And not so.

For so long
I put off coming to Thee
In the pure intimacy
Of absolute honesty.
Kneeling
Only in visibility.
I avoided Thee
Thinking I must first destroy
The not so good
In me.
Deeming it evil,
Wrong,
Bad.
I found the fight
Futile.

I could not destroy
Any part of me—
Not my anger,
Nor my selfishness,
Nor my hunger to be
Significant.

And so,
humbled to the depths
Of my own
Powerlessness
I came to Thy true altar
Invisible,
With these indivisible things.
And there I found
What I had never before
Supposed.
Thou hast not
Destroyed them in me,
either.

Thou hast purged them,
Not from me,
But from iniquity.

Dear God,
I laid them all before Thee,
And Thou hast made
A daughter of me.

In the Light of My Closet: Confessions of a Mormon Mystic

Entering my undergrad class in English Literature never failed to warp my sense of time. While I sat there, enthralled, an hour would go by in what seemed like five minutes. However, on the day I learned I was a mystic, time stood stark still, allowing the recognition of a truth to flood through me—so powerful that tears spilled down my cheeks. I often wonder what the other students—most of them in their twenties—thought of the old, graying lady, who sat in the back of the class, frequently crying.

On that particular day, we discussed the life of John Donne. Through his poetry we traced his wild, lustful, bawdy youth, then his transformation in mid-life to what became in his full maturity, a complete consecration of his life to God. Here was a soul, like my own, who tried the world's ways and found them vaporous, without hope and without substance. I felt the resonance begin. I identified deeply with Donne's "Johnny-come-lately" metamorphosis, having myself only truly been converted *to Christ* in the last six years of my thirty years as a Mormon. I was pulled from my reverie. The professor, speaking of Donne's degree of amazing—even mighty—change, used the word "mystic."

"By the time he died, John Donne had become one of the greatest Christian mystics in the history of English literature," he said.

I cringed. *Mystic?* How could the professor use language like that in a BYU classroom?! Didn't he realize that in our culture the word "mystic" was an epithet, a profanity?

Dabbing my eyes with a damp ball of Kleenex, I nursed my shock by reminding myself that, after all, this was the "infamous" BYU *English* Department, a chronic battleground of ideology and interpretation, not only of literature, but of life. A person was apt to learn *anything* here. For example, I already learned that besides being a Mormon woman, wife, and mother, I was also and simultaneously an *idealist*, a *romantic*, and a *transcendentalist*—which, taken all together, explained perfectly why I *was* a Mormon woman, wife, and mother.

Even so, these self-discoveries took me far afield from my previous life of domesticity, of cooking, canning, cleaning and crafts—enticing me to love ideas and thoughts and words and the life of the mind as much as I ever loved the work of my hands. Already, my housecleaning schedule was several seasons behind and I had reduced my traditional fall canning to a tenth of what it once was—from forty bushels to four. It was probably best to leave this mystic stuff alone—no matter how it called to me.

But the witness of the Spirit of Truth would not let me ignore the *fact* that I identified from the farthest reaches of my soul—the part of me that Elizabeth Barrett Browning spoke of as "the depths and breadth and height my soul can feel when reaching out of sight"—with John Donne's poetry, filled with intense and passionate consecration to Christ. I could not deny that I felt, when studying Donne's life experience, the same transformation I so recently experienced in myself. I felt in Donne a kindred spirit—someone who, as President Ezra Taft Benson once put it, "choose[s] to follow [Christ], be changed for Him, captained by

Him, consumed in Him, and born again."[1] That's what Donne had lived. That's what I was living.

The professor called the converted, reborn Donne a *mystic*. How could this consummate love of Christ be connected with the concept of "Mysticism" as found in the Topical Guide in the Standard Works of the Church? "**Mysticism**: *see* False Doctrine; Sorcery; Superstitions; Traditions of Men" (p.335). I had to find out what the dissonance between my sincere love of the Savior and the words in the Topical Guide meant.

As I prayed about this concept of mysticism, I was led to remember that in the weakness of our language (which can also be its strength) the same word can have different meanings, depending on the context (time and place) in which it is used. I felt impressed to look for further elucidation of "mystic" in my dictionary. To my surprise and delight I found these two definitions, both devoid of any reference to sorcery or superstitions:

> The experience of mystical union or direct communion with ultimate reality.
>
> The belief that direct knowledge of God, spiritual truth or ultimate reality can be attained through subjective experience. (*Merriam Webster Collegiate Dictionary*, 10th Edition)

Wait a minute!

There was no dissonance here! The resonance was back. So was the burning witness of "ultimate reality," at least as *I* sincerely perceived it: direct knowledge of God, spiritual truth *and* ultimate reality can be attained through subjective (i.e. personal, singular, one-on-one) experience! This was something I already knew, and I had learned it *by studying the theology—the teachings—of Mormonism concerning God.*

Of course! And why not? Wasn't this very concept—this belief that *direct knowledge of God*, spiritual truth or ultimate reality can be attained through *subjective* experience—the very heart and core of Mormonism? Didn't the prophet Joseph Smith himself utter these words:

> So it was with me. I had actually seen a light, and in the midst of that light I saw two Personages, and they did in reality speak to me...For I had seen a vision; I knew it, and I knew that God knew it, and I could not deny it, neither dared I do it... (*Pearl of Great Price,* Joseph Smith History 1:25.)

Again, wasn't it Joseph who also said:

> For God hath not revealed anything to Joseph, but what he will make known unto the Twelve, and even the least Saint may know all things as fast as he is able to bear them. For the day must come when no man need say to his neighbor know ye the Lord for all shall know him (who Remain) from the least to the greatest. (Joseph Smith as recorded by Willard Richards, *Writings of the Prophet Joseph Smith,* ed. Andrew F. Ehat and Lyndon W. Cook. p.4)

Joseph not only claimed to have "direct knowledge of God, spiritual truth, or ultimate reality" for himself, but was offering to share the same experience—in other words, the life of a *mystic*—with even the least Saint, as soon as they were ready. Think of it! He was trying to create a whole church of *saints*, a population of prophets, a people endowed with an apostolic degree of "subjective experience" with a living, loving, *available* God.

ℒ

My first sense of the mystical life, though of course I didn't know what to call it back then, came to me at about five years of age, during the hours I spent in sequestered chambers I created for myself by crawling around and around in the three-foot-tall spring grass in the fields near my parents' house. After constructing the safe parameters of my cloister, I would flop down on my back and while chewing on a stalk of sweet grass, stare up at the cobalt blue sky above me. Today, I can't imagine what I was thinking—or probably *not* thinking—about all the little creatures that shared my refuge—the grasshoppers, ants, spiders and the occasional lizard or snake. Fortunately, most of the time my fellow inconsequential creatures tried to stay as clear of me as I did of them.

Already seeking that Something I could feel pulsating in and through *all things*, I didn't go out into the fields to commiserate with other life forms which, like myself, no one gave more than minimal thought to. Instead, I sought that environment because in its ignored and abandoned peace, I found my first awareness of heaven since falling to Earth.

There, in those sacred, private places I imagined being loved, cherished. I played for hours at a family life I had never experienced but only glimpsed in my friends' homes—a life made safe by a caring mother, a loving father, and a sibling or two who found security and nurturance in each other. In awful contrast, in the private hell of my own household, I witnessed and experienced the crushing weight of my father's disdain and outright disgust towards my mother—and by association toward me, the not-a-son-but-a-girl-child mistakenly conceived by this conniving woman. I lived and breathed the total degradation of anything feminine, anything female, my particular brand of "I-am-ness." Self-loathing became riveted upon my heart by every kind of abuse: emotional, verbal, physical, and sexual. In their drunken self-absorption, my parents thought no more of me being in the room than a night-stand or chest of drawers if they wanted to get naked and sexual. And if my mother was too drunk and my father wanted some sexual favor, I was often recruited.

Out in the fields, from April to October, I played from early morning to late in the evening. Sometimes I brought my toy horses and cowboy figures into the fields, and my little private world became even more micro. The grass served as tall forests or jungles where I carved out corrals and homesteads for my little champions of heroism and truth. Being a child of the 50's, I was enthralled with Davy Crockett, Roy Rogers, and the "Masked Man." My heart resonated to this paradigm of male nobility and goodness. It felt like sweet balm to my otherwise male-battered female soul.

Some nights—especially in the summer—when my parents left me alone while they went "next door" to visit (the nearest house was at least the length of a football field from ours), or when they weren't sober enough to notice whether I was alive or dead, much less in or out of bed, I would haul a blanket and pillow out onto the lawn and lie on my back and let the infinite come down out of the stars and cover me, lie with me, come into me so gently. No groping, no force. Soft, as if every pore of my body were access enough to my soul. I was loved and I knew it. I needed no mother, father, sister, or brother to tell me so. The UNKNOWN GOD who Paul preached to the men of Athens introduced Himself to me long before I knew His name, or knew that it was by His name I would be called (Mosiah 5:7).

℘

In my eighth year, as my father fought and lost a brief battle with cancer, I found myself living with the family of one of his close work associates, first for weekends and then for weeks. Devoutly Catholic, they enrolled me in catechism classes. They assumed my father, who was raised a strict Irish Catholic, wouldn't mind. They were right. He didn't mind, not so much for religious reasons, but because he was very distracted in the five months it took him to go from robust, bawdy health to imminent death.

The teachings I received in those catechism classes were my first exposure to Christ. I recognized Him immediately as the hero, the balm, the infinite that came down out of the stars and loved me. Sitting in class every Saturday morning, I prepared for what the nuns insisted would be my "First Communion," but I knew better. I tried to tell them so. I asked questions and offered answers that weren't in the printed catechism, that didn't fit in the black and white world of my traditionally attired teachers. Consequently, I spent more and more of my catechism study sitting out on the back steps of the tiny parish, banished from the classroom for being "disruptive." I was okay with that; it was spring and there were ants and grasshoppers to watch.

Disruptive or not, the sisters recognized I was a child obviously in need of religion and salvation. Stretching and bending the requirements as far as they could to fit me in, they finally prevailed on the presiding priest to let me take my first communion that Easter. I was thrilled. I could think of nothing more wonderful than dressing up in an eight-year-old's version of bridal attire and approaching the altar of Christ to partake of the emblems of His flesh and blood and offer Him my life in return—heart, might, mind and strength.

I did receive my first communion that Easter day, but not in the morning mass as planned. In the morning service, kneeling on the padded bar attached to the pew ahead of me, surrounded by a couple dozen other little brides, all in white dresses and veils, I swooned in a fashion that would have done Julian of Norwich, Margery Kempe or Teresa of Jesus proud. Apparently, none of the nuns there at St. Francis' little Catholic chapel knew much of their own religious heritage. I was half-walked, half-carried out of the mass and did not approach the altar to receive the Eucharist until later that afternoon, after my garments were scrubbed clean of any sign of the blood that had dripped from my skinned nose.

The afternoon service was sort of anticlimactic, actually. There was no early morning sunshine flowing through the humble-but-sincere stained glass windows along the east side of the room; there was no smell of fresh little girls, be-ribboned and be-netted, bowed and curled, perfumed and prepared. Then again, now that I think about it, it might have been the very presence of all those elements that contributed to my faint, earlier. Maybe it was the beauty of the sunshine and the aura in the room that morning that caused me to hold my breath too often, too long in sheer awe of the presence of God. It would be many years before I learned of the examples of King Lamoni's father and Alma the Younger, both overwhelmed physically by the experience of coming to God.

The first two years after my father's death, after my mother recklessly spent his insurance benefits, we moved every couple of months to avoid paying rent. With each move, the house or apartment got shabbier and the neighborhood rougher, until we were living in a part of North Sacramento relegated to migrant farm workers and practicing alcoholics. Here, the people either worked all day at hard labor or slept all day so they could drink all night. My mother did some of both. I went to school, between bouts with infectious hepatitis and my mother's "boyfriends." Even though I was only eleven and twelve, I knew one thing for sure: these were neither *boys* nor *friends*. I have memories of successfully fending off multiple advances. I have post-traumatic stress disorder symptoms to remind me of the times I wasn't successful.

Though I never made it back to church after my First Communion, I continued the practice of formal prayer, on my knees before God. I started with the memorized prayers on the rosary which I had learned in catechism. Always, *always*, though, somewhere into the process I ceased to pray someone else's words and began to use my own. My prayers dissolved into gut-wrenching, heart-breaking, soul-cleansing exchanges between my

Lord and me. Some nights I fell into bed, exhausted from pleading with Him to restore my life to some degree of sanity, security, stability—all the time picturing real homes, adequate food, clean drinking water, new clothes, a mother and a father living together peacefully under the same roof. Instead of this, however, He gave me Himself in the form of an undeniable witness of His reality and His loving availability to me. I knew I was in the presence of a living entity, kneeling by me, sitting by me, lying by me, holding me in invisible arms of tangible, rational love. Day after day, night after night, I survived, walking and talking with my God who had now become my dearest counselor and friend. Through Him I found sanity in insanity and sanctification in hell.

☙

Somewhere in my thirteenth year, two monumental influences converged in my life that eclipsed my spiritual experiences and left me groping in the dark.

After creeping up gradually in the previous two years, puberty hit full force. Since the age of twelve, I had been developing breasts, establishing my monthly cycle, hating and dreading every moment of it. I watched how men leered at developed breasts. A woman ceased to have any hope of having a face as soon as she grew a bosom. She ceased to have a voice as soon as she could moan unintelligibly in the midst of intercourse. At least that's what I observed watching my mother interact with men. In my thirteenth year I found myself with interests and longings that perplexed and confused me all at the same time. Despite my fears of the opposite sex, I found myself drawn toward them, enjoying them, wanting their attention and company. Desperately, I sought for moorings on this slippery slope. What could I grasp onto to save me from the heart-sickening life my mother lived?

At the same time, my prayers were changing. Not only was I feeling less childlike towards males in general, but also toward God, who had always been male to me, though His comfort resonated with the definite echoes of a mother's tenderness. How could I talk to Him without reservation about these feelings I was having toward the masculine—these longings? I couldn't. The conversational, best-friend intimacy of my innocent childhood became eclipsed by my need for a lover. I couldn't begin to conceptualize my dilemma, much less unravel it and lay it straight. All I knew for certain was, I fell into these confusions and fears and began to delete more and more of my truth from my prayers. My relationship with my sweet God was no longer whole. It was compartmentalized, fragmented. I began to pray selectively, half-heartedly. Previous tender impressions and feelings from Him came less and less frequently. In truth, it was I who was backing away from our previous level of trust and communion. Prayer became a reluctant, uncomfortable chore.

It was in this state of half-hearted, half-attentive relationship with the Highest, the Divine, the Truth, that His companionship became garbled and overshadowed by what I found in "romance" magazines and a handful of sexually explicit novels. The more I read, the more I wanted what I read. Still I was terrified of reliving my mother's life. At least in this terror I found an undeniable need to pray about something, though my prayers were not as before. It wasn't Him and me anymore—not in fields, not in star-filled skies, not in solitary bedrooms, kneeling by or lying upon my bed. I wouldn't let Him that close. I fell into a desperate need, or so I thought, to be loved by someone besides Him. But what could I do about it? I *knew* if I didn't allow Him in my life, I would be without sanity in the insane world I had grown up in; I would be sucked into my mother's "tradition." I would have multiple partners—one-night stands, week long affairs. I would become a misogynist the equal of any and all of my partners put together.

In the midst of this paradoxical combination of need and fear, my prayers were reduced to rote actions once more. I repeated the same prayer over and over again, driven not by faith in Him but by fear of men and of myself. "God, what can I do? Please save me. Please show me what to do."

One day, on an ever-so-lonely fall afternoon, I flipped the old black and white television from channel to channel to channel— all three of them—looking for something to do besides my homework. I had come home from school to an empty house. I had no idea where my mother and her current live-in boyfriend were. He had gotten paid last Friday—it was now Monday—and they had gone out for some "groceries" and hadn't come back since. Usually, they'd come home by Sunday to sleep off enough of their drunk to go to work the next morning. But not this weekend. I had no idea why. I didn't dare call the police for fear they would come and take me away from my mother. So I cleaned house, ate what I could find, and waited.

As I flipped through the channels every half-hour, I watched cartoons, *Gilligan's Island*, the evening news, *Rawhide*, and finally the *Monday Night Movies*. The featured movie was *The Nun's Story* with Audrey Hepburn. That caught my attention. I had never been able to forget the fascination I felt for the sisters who taught me catechism. There was something about them, despite their reaction to my spontaneous questions—or maybe *because* of their response—that struck me as absolute and secure. They seemed absolutely committed, absolutely safe in their black and white world. Maybe this movie would give me some insight into why these flesh and blood women seemed so aloof from the cares and ills of this world.

As I watched the movie, I was caught up in the main character's reasons for seeking the life of a nun: her intense love of God, her longing to be free of the heartbreak of this world. I sat transfixed, weeping the first heart-deep tears I had shed in months as she took her vows of celibacy and poverty. *That*. *That* was how much I wanted to give to God. *That* was how much I wanted to love Him.

As they placed a ring on her finger and declared her His bride, I lay down on the floor and wept uncontrollably, inconsolably. I knew He was willing to be as a loving husband to me. I knew I had to take sacred vows, wear sacred, symbolic clothing and wear a ring symbolizing my covenant of consecration to Him. I knew my body and mind were sacred gifts from Him to be offered back to Him. Once again, by a mystical experience—deeply spiritual, deeply personal—I was saved from drowning in the toxic waste of my surroundings; saved *by* God and *for* God to live a life consecrated to Him and His work and glory. Knowing no other example of such a complete giving up of one's life to God, I was sure I was being called to become a nun.

The only problem with becoming a Catholic nun, or a Catholic anything for that matter, was it had been five years and ten neighborhoods since my catechism and First Communion. I hadn't attended a religious service of any kind in all those years. I had no idea where to go, no way or means to go there. However, I had a more convenient way of cloistering myself and coming to God—I discovered I could write. I could put down on paper the "music" in my head, the response in my heart to the life I was living.

I had been an insatiable reader since about age seven. I remember reading *Alice in Wonderland* and *Through the Looking Glass* before my eighth birthday, before my father died. And though I didn't understand Lewis Carroll's political intentions, I sensed the allegory to life and to life's real characters. I read fantasies and fairy tales. I read dog and horse stories, mysteries and romances, historic fiction like *The Agony and the Ecstasy*, *The Big Fisherman*. I read biographies of Rodin and Tolstoy. These and myriad other books were one of my favorite escapes from the otherwise pointless, irrational, mindless world of being my mother's child. They were my retreat. But my own writing was my holy place, my place of prayer and communion with the truth, of sanity and of hope, of imagination, both fantastic and Divine.

By the time I finished eighth grade, I had written a dozen personal essays, a handful of short stories, several dozen poems and a novella of 115 pages. Unfortunately, most of these papers were lost in one of our quick moves to avoid yet another irate landlord wanting the last two months' rent. A cardboard box was left behind and no one dared or cared enough to go back to get it. I always wondered if anyone looked in it before they tossed it in the trash. "Just a bunch of papers," they might have said.

Ø

"So what do you think about marriage?" It seemed like a legit-imate enough question to ask a friend I'd known for nearly a year, especially one who carried my books home from school every day. After all, we shared the same homeroom table, lunch hour, second period algebra, and last period mechanical drawing. I think it was the mechanical drawing class that did it, that made it safe for a girl to ask a boy such a question. He continued walking along beside me, carrying our books together and limping along, one foot in the gutter and one on the sidewalk—a strange combination of chivalry and klutziness.

"I'm not getting married until I get back from my mission," he answered without looking up.

"Mission? What's a mission?" I listened as he told me about his church and how young men go on missions when they're nineteen and teach investigators for two years.

"And then, when I get home, I'll be able to get married in the temple for eternity."

"In the temple? What's a temple?" And before he could answer, I added, already beginning to feel the fire, the breathless-ness, "You believe in getting married for *eternity*?"

Those were only the first of many questions I plied him with. Every day I asked him more. He told me about temple marriage, about being sealed to your partner for time *and eternity*. Somewhere in one of our conversations he even told me about the sacred temple garment you wore for the rest of your life, to symbolize your covenants with God. I was desperate to hear more. Could I learn more about his church? Who did I need to talk to? He said he'd ask his mom.

Days later, a woman called, introducing herself as "Sister Perry." She was a "stake missionary," calling to see if I would like to set up an appointment to meet the full-time missionaries at her home next Monday night. (This was in the pre-family home evening era.) I was a little shaken by the use of the word "sister," having only one previous exposure to the use of the term in a religious setting. I wondered if she wore a habit. Sister Perry offered to come to my house and pick me up on the scheduled evening. Reluctantly, I agreed. I was deeply ashamed of the "poor white trash" appearance of the neighborhood we lived in, but nothing could compete with the need I felt from deep inside to learn more about this church that taught that all men and women—not just priests and nuns—could dress in sacred robes and be married for all eternity—and to each other, besides! That was exactly the degree of honor I longed to see in the male/female relationship. I gave her my address.

On that first night with the missionaries I fell madly in love, both with what they were teaching me and with them. If this is what going on a mission turned boys into—these fresh, clean-cut, dashing, sparkling, gorgeous creatures—I already had my friend's farewell, homecoming, *and wedding* planned.

The evening went like a dream for me and for the elders. I was a "golden contact." I ate up every word they said and wept when they pulled the foundation of Christ out from under the church structure on the flannel board, making the whole thing fall to the floor. Now I realized how it was that the only church I had ever known had a semblance of the truth, but not the fullness thereof. God didn't want just select individuals to dedicate their lives to Him. He wanted the entire membership to be that devoted. This entire Church was His, preparing to be His Bride.

I'm not sure how or where I got that message. I don't think it was something one of those cute boys—sorry, it's the hormones—said that night, even though they did give me two lessons in one sitting and sent me home with a *Book of Mormon* and a copy of *A Marvelous Work and a Wonder*. I devoured *A Marvelous Work*, got thirty pages into the *Book of Mormon,* and asked for baptism at our next lesson, two nights later. They inquired about my mother. Would she be willing to sign a permission slip for my baptism? I didn't know how to tell them that the problem with getting my mother to sign something was not whether she would, but whether she could, and how long it might be before I could catch her in that brief interval between shaking with withdrawals and being too drunk to write legibly.

I prayed to God for a miracle, and it happened. I found her sober enough to sign. I was baptized the next Saturday night, five days after hearing the first discussion. There were five people there—the two full-time elders whose names I have forgotten; Sister Perry (I found out she didn't wear a habit); Brother Larsen, another stake missionary; and the custodian who opened the building, filled the font, and emptied it when we were through. Mine was the only baptism that night. I don't remember music or talks, though I imagine there were some. I do remember coming out of the water, *knowing* I was clean, searingly aware of my innocence before God. I remember the hands on my wet head, the words "I confirm you a member of The Church of Jesus Christ of Latter-day Saints" and "receive the Holy Ghost."

First thing the next morning, I availed myself of my new church membership by showing up at early morning seminary to begin a lifetime of gospel study under the tutelage of many fine teachers. I eventually achieved 100% attendance at seminary, four-

year graduation from the Institute of Religion, twenty-years of pilgrimages to BYU for Education Week, a variety of home study
classes—all on top of the weekly routine of Gospel Doctrine and
Relief Society lessons. Still, it would take me twenty-five years and
the lessons of Job before I appreciated the fullness of the Gift of
the Holy Ghost, of the First Comforter—to know the living reality
of the Second Comforter.

$$\mathscr{D}$$

About a year after my John Donne inspired epiphany, the
concept of mysticism came up again, this time in a Masters level
class on rhetoric. Someone read a selection from the writings of a
woman, Teresa of Avila, identifying her as a sixteenth-century
Catholic mystic. As the rest of the rhetoric class went on to
consider other quotes from other sources, I sat transfixed by the
quotes from Teresa. They pierced me even more than Donne's.
Immediately the burning started again and, as if this wave of
witness only recalled and intensified the first, I could not avoid the
truth. At least in the privacy of my own mind, I had to admit it:
I'm one of these people. But who are they? I mean *we*. I mean *me*?

Sorcerers?

I still worried over the synonyms used in the Topical Guide.

I didn't feel much like a sorcerer. I turned inward, searching
my soul.

No. No sorcery here. Just the life of a forty-five-year-old
woman, divested of all tradition-based respect and social system
support, demoted from the second pew in the chapel at Sacrament
services to the back row of the overflow section. A woman struggling desperately with poverty while trying to follow the witness
of the Spirit of the Lord, as best she discerns it, to prepare for a

vocation, rather than opting to be a working-woman at a nine-to-five service-sector job.

Apparently, God's time for me to own my reality was quickening, because it was not long before the confirming witness came that convicted me, in an irrefutable way, of mysticism. Only a few weeks later, one of my favorite diversions on campus—hanging out with the books in the BYU bookstore—led me on a "wander" into the "General Religion" section. Browsing through the bookstore was the cheapest therapy I could imagine. I was constantly amazed at how much better I knew myself by keeping track of the books I would buy, *if I could*. That day I found Teresa's autobiography: *The Life of Teresa of Jesus*.

Or had it found me?

Teresa of Jesus. Of Jesus.

I paid for it with my whole month's lunch allowance.

I purchased it and took it home.

Or was I the purchased one, being taken home?

I knew I could not casually read this book. I knew I would find words pouring out of my soul in response to this book. Teresa *of Jesus*. To be called by His name. I knew what that felt like. What had it felt like for her?

Just a quick glance at the introduction affected my pulse, my rate of breathing and my sense of time. I felt, as Madeleine L'Engle would put it, that I was experiencing a "wrinkle in time."[2] This book wasn't just *for* me, it was *about* me. Her words could have been my own!

> I was...ashamed to go to my confessor...for fear he might laugh at me and say: 'What a Saint Paul she is, with her heavenly visions.'

...for it is love that speaks, and my soul is so far transported that I take no notice of the distance that separates it from God.

And she scribbles at breakneck speed and with tremendous intensity, never revising her work or even rereading it to see what she has said last.

Her mind was so completely immersed in Biblical phraseology that it is sometimes hard to tell if she is consciously quoting at all. (E. Allison Peers, trans., ed., *The Life of Teresa of Jesus*. New York:Doubleday, 1991. pp. 17, 20, 18, 24)

With the book in my hands, I rushed to the library to find an empty carrel in a deserted corner where I could cloister myself and write in my journal. Writing with abandon, I recorded my soul-deep response to Teresa's life and writings:

Now I have read a few more pages of Teresa's and I am in tears. How can this be; how can she be quoting from my most private journals, hundreds of years before I was born? Oh Lord! How I have longed to hear this kind of living witness of Thee from the lips of another woman. If this is mysticism, then burn me at the stake. I'm a mystic.

A few pages later in Teresa's book I continued to write in mine:

You know, there was a time when I seriously thought mystical was the same as "mythical"—as in fairies and sprites. But fairies and sprites aren't real and I am definitely real. Here I sit writing. I look around me, though, in the here and now of my life, and I see no one with whom to relate or identify—not this deeply, anyway. I know no one who will admit that God is to them a living presence, who shares conversation with Him at the veil, frequently, just as the temple teaches we can. I find no one willing to admit that, like me, they walk in the spirit by nature, and in the world as a slightly lonely apparition. Once again, I have to cry out, Why? Why did He put me here in the midst of Mormonism? We have such a tradition of veiling or hiding spiritual experiences. Yet we are supposed to be Saints. A whole church of Saints. A whole church of Josephs? Of Teresas?

As I read on in Teresa's life story, it became more and more obvious that in tone, essence, spirit, intensity, and sincerity, her life and mine were interchangeable. And like Joseph, I knew that God knew that *I* knew it, and I could not deny it. A few nights later, I wrote in the same little notebook,

The energy that is released into my life by acknowledging this truth about myself is almost more than I can bear alone. I picture taking this book to someone and laying it open and saying, "Read." I struggle to fill in the details of that picture without fear.

Who? Who would I share this with? Who could I come out of my closet and tell? Who in Mormon-dom? No wonder I fantasize about returning to Catholicism. At least there I could be myself out loud. Here, so many are afraid. I have kept this light turned down in my life for as long as I can endure. In desperation I have taken to writing nearly every morning from three to six A.M. I need no alarm clock. My heart and mind wake up to a call, to an eagerness, that seems to pass both ways between God and me.

During these times of writing I feel like I have finally turned up the light. I feel like the eagle found and rescued from a chicken coop full of eagles who still

think they're chickens. God takes me to a mountaintop and holds me up to the heavens and says, in spirit and in truth, "Thou art an eagle, now fly." And I do, every morning. I spread my wings, ride the winds of God and soar overhead as Israel lies sleeping with dawn at our doors. Don't we realize it will stay dark until we awaken to who and what we are?

Sacred garments, sacred covenants, consecrated lives. Latter-day Saints. A nation of priests and priestesses, prophets and prophetesses.

Lord, there I go again, seeing too far. I'm too high. Too high. It is all true. Too true. I tuck in my wings. But it's too late. I saw. I know the truth of who and what I am. Now, to reconcile that with where I am.

Since this first exposure to the life and writings of Teresa of Jesus, I was led, not knowing beforehand what to expect, into a class on Women's *Meditational* Literature. There, we studied literature produced by women as a form of meditation, created by women who felt called *directly* by God and who, whether in the cloister or not, lived their lives "consumed in Christ." As I read works by not only Teresa, but also by St. Perpetua, Hadewigch of Brabent, Julian of Norwich, Margery Kempe and Amelia Lanyer, I was astounded to find a body of literature as rich in testimony as any left by the male voices preserved in holy writ. It was as if I were hearing a descant, sung high and pure in tone, above the deep sounds of the brethren. Women have been recording their spiritual experiences with God all through the centuries! This literary tradition exists—*outside* my voluminous journals and notebooks! My heart wanted to leap for joy. I had come home! I had come home! I wasn't crazy! And I wasn't alone. I was and am part of a tradition—an old and venerable tradition—women writing about, to *and for* God.

𝒟

It's 5:03 A.M. I look down at my fingers moving on the keys in the pale electronic glow of my monitor. My hands and arms cast distinct shadows to my left as they interrupt the yellower, warmer beam of the incandescent bulb shining out of my walk-in closet, where only a few minutes ago I held sweet communion with God. And now, steadied by the powerful renewal of security afforded me in that communion, I give myself permission to "hang out on the page"[3] as Julia Cameron would say. I am ready to go where the truth leads me—into the depths of my psyche, my soul. I have less than two months until my masters thesis must be finished. My fingertips rest on the keys as I close my eyes and take a deep breath, preparing myself to "drop down the well."[4] The steady whirring of my hard drive takes on a barely perceptible rhythm when I close my eyes. "Writing is about *hearing*," Julia wrote. I hold my breath and try to be only my ears, hearing. I am amazed to find that the sound of the computer actually pulsates "around" and "in and out" at the same time…as if it were…as if it were *purring*!

As if my metaphor for the computer has given off some sort of beckoning energy, I hear a scratch at my closed bedroom door. It's my cat, Squat, directing me to let him out of the house for his morning rounds. Unlike my computer, he doesn't wait for my commands, he gives them. In build, he's a rather unusual cat. Short legged, low to the ground, broad, stubby…in a word, squat. But in temperament and social graces (or lack of), he's your archetypal cat.

As I obediently open my bedroom door to acknowledge his imperative presence, I notice the kitchen light shining into the semi-dark hallway. Apparently, it has burned all night.

I'm not surprised or disturbed. The fact is, there's always a light burning through the night at our house. Kitchen or bathroom or hallway—sometimes all three. As you can imagine, my electric bill is fearsome. But then, what else can you expect when you're running a lighthouse for lost children, adrift in the night? Bruised and broken-hearted children. Frowning, fierce-eyed children, holed-up inside bodies grown tall, grown round, grown hard. Child-warriors, full of anger that I helped provoke during those years when I knew not Christ—when I only belonged to His Church, but not *to Him*. Children who have taken their abuse into their own hands, who do whatever they can to fill in the confused, aching void I riveted upon their hearts by the lies I modeled for them.

I walk down the hall, towards the shadowy front room. I pass the brightly lit kitchen on my left without reaching for the light switch; I turn right and descend the stairs into the dark entry. The burned-out light in the entry hangs twelve feet above the floor, enclosed in a white sphere covered with a year's dust. I haven't had the time, money or motivation to change the bulb or even clean the globe.

Opening the unlocked front door of my home, I stand in the doorway for a minute or two. I live in one of the few places in the United States where a person can still leave their front door unlocked all night and have even half a hope of being un-robbed, un-mugged, and still alive in the morning. The refreshing morning air swirls around my legs and bare arms. Even though it's the second week in September and the whole Wasatch front is trembling between summer and fall, summer is hanging on. I watch Squat scurry away into the bushes along the front of the house before I look toward the approaching dawn beginning to outline the mountaintops to the east. One lone car passes through the intersection at the east end of our street, just three houses away. From the west, I hear the footfalls of an early morning jogger coming around the corner at the other end of our block. It's a cookie-cutter morning in the perfect grid of my Utah neighborhood.

I close the door quietly. I climb slowly up the entry stairs and pass into that hole in time that has permanently attached itself to that particular spot in my house. Once more, I am seeing the highway patrolman's sober, almost rigid expression. I hear again his tight, carefully rehearsed words, the flattened sound of his tone: "I regret to inform you,... inform you... inform you,... that your daughter,... your daughter,... daughter,... daughter... daughter...

The words reverberate through my soul, through the room, through my life, through the earth...and continue to restore me to the one scrape of sanity, the one certainty I cling to—the fact that God didn't put me in control of anyone else's agency but my own.

Though it seems like I've climbed forever, it is really only a few moments later that I emerge from the vortex of that hole and gain the top of the stairs. Before turning to flee toward my bedroom, I grip the black wrought-iron railing and carefully scan the several couches and chairs in my spacious front room. I study the shadows in the corners of the room; I never know which of my children I will find sleeping where. They could be anywhere, curled up in a sleeping bag or blanket, like exhausted, homeless refugees despite the roof over their heads. Though there are six bedrooms in the house, I can never count on them being used by the child assigned to them, or by any child, for that matter. The cat usually has his pick of empty beds.

Julia, my youngest—an eleven-year-old daughter—often sleeps near me, on my bed. I say "on" rather than "in," because I have tried to encourage her to stay in her own bed by refusing to allow her to get into bed with me, under the covers. Besides, sleeping with her is like sleeping with a windmill. Still, I can't refuse her when she comes during the night, dragging her own "Lion King" quilt and pillow, crawling up on the empty side of my queen-size bed. She's there now with her back turned to the light and to the sounds of my morning vigil.

My next two children just older than her are both boys, Matthew and Derek. While they each have a bed here in this house, they choose to spend most of their time at their father's squalid apartment. Though I have full legal custody of my children, I have found I have no more control of them now than I had before my divorce. In fact I have less. If I do not cooperate with their demands, or if I try to enforce any of my own, they simply make a phone call, flip me off and wait on the corner for their dad to come rescue them from "the b—." It seems their father's $100,000 annual income and total lack of discipline appeals to them at thirteen and fifteen in much the same way that "Donkey-Island" appealed to Pinocchio and his pals. You can see why, when you consider that in my home we get by on $14,000 a year and require everyone to take responsibility without compensation. Still, I keep the lights burning for them, just in case some real or remembered night-time horror drives them out of their father's "employ."

The fourth bed belongs to Debra, my seventeen-year-old daughter. She hardly ever uses it—mainly because I won't let her bring home the people she sleeps with. When she does make it home, she doesn't get as far as her bedroom before she crashes into a drug-induced, coma-like sleep. Most mornings, if she's here at all, I find her in front of the TV, sprawled half-on, half-off the couch. I fetch a blanket or sheet and tuck it around her sleeping body, along with prayers of gratitude that she is still here, on this side of the veil, where I can see her and touch her. When she wakes, our worlds return to opposite corners of the universe, locked behind walls of anger, blame, and shame so thick I can't begin to reach her. In fact, any interaction with me sets her spinning off into space even further. I live in constant, aching fear that one of these nights she will fall through a black hole and never return, like Karen did. The combination of these realities makes living with her feel as if I am sitting a few feet away from someone poised on the edge of the seventeenth floor of a high-rise building, ready to jump. The last thing I dare do is make any overt move toward her. Instead, I try to be still and *listen*.

Listening, I hear God counsel me to leave my doors as well as my heart unlocked, to not fear the electric bill, to allow my sons to have their choice, and to look to my *Savior*, Jesus Christ, for strength and patience to endure Debra's lifestyle. Obeying this counsel, merciful and illogical as it may seem, I find myself in a place of peace that makes no sense, and I find the power to face my life-in-the-last-days challenges without numbing myself with Prozac or Twinkies. I am comforted by His words as they come into my mind, words of mercy and forgiveness for both myself and my children. Encircled in the arms of His all-encompassing and comprehending love, I can face the truth about how I parented in the past without dying of shame or resorting to blame. And while sorrow walks with me continually, I am not depressed or frozen with fear of continuing on with my own life. Miraculously, I continue to awake nearly every morning around four without an alarm clock, responding instead to that still, small voice, the one Samuel first mistook as Eli's, inviting me to my closet. There, I find refuge in a private holy-of-holies, attended by the presence of my beloved Savior and dearest Friend. As one with Joseph Smith and Sidney Rigdon, I emerge from my closet, as they did from the Kirtland temple, empowered by "the testimony,...that he lives!" (D&C 76:22)

Finding no children asleep in the living room, I return down the hallway to my bedroom and sit once again at my computer desk, bathed in the light from my closet. Beyond my window blinds, the diffused light of approaching day is washing the darkness out of the sky and landscape. It will be another hour before colors begin to emerge, but there's no stopping it—the sun is returning.

I have to smile at the meaning of the currently popular expression, "to come out of the closet," or in other words, to reveal some deep, life-shaking secret about one's self. In recent years more and more Mormons have been doing that—coming out of their "closet" and admitting previously hidden truths about themselves. Many have admitted they are deeply depressed, overwhelmed by the accumulating stresses and heartaches of life in the latter-days. Others are admitting they don't really *know* the Church is what it claims, or even that there is a God. Others are abandoning commitments to spouses and children. Some have admitted they are homosexual. Others are coming out and revealing childhoods ravaged by severe trauma—sexual abuse, physical and emotional violence—trauma that no amount of activity in Church, no amount of their own desperately good works, has healed.

I feel a burning and a swelling all the way from my throat to my solar plexis. My breath catches in awe of the testimony sweeping through me—that I, too, must come out of my closet and tell my whole truth. I must tell it for the sake of those who are finally admitting theirs. Like them, I must stop fearing the repercussions I may face. I must tell the world what I've learned about the Mormon Church by living in it, participating in its ordinances and searching out its precepts: It is *true*. In other words, it is telling the truth. It is what it claims to be. It is a world-class religion, as deep and wide and high as the infinite love and mercy of Christ upon which it is founded.

I must tell the whole truth and I have to confess *in public*, no matter the consequences: I've tried Mormonism in the crucible of abject and total moral, emotional, and spiritual devastation, and have *not* found it wanting. Yes, you heard me correctly. That's the secret I practice in my closet: *Mormonism works*. It has the power to deliver exactly what Joseph Smith promised and modeled: the most profound and yet practical expression of Christian *mysticism* ever known on earth.

Ø

I raise the blinds at the window over my art table so I can watch the sunrise reflecting from the mountains on the west side of the valley. At the very tips of the Oquirrh Mountains the dawn begins. Their tops are torches set on fire by the sun's first rays as they peek over the ridges of the Wasatch Mountains on the east of the valley. The valley itself, is still in shadow.

I lean my forehead against the cool glass and close my eyes. "Lord, there I go again, seeing too far. I'm too high. Too high. But it's true. It's all true. The gospel is true. So true. I tuck in my wings. But it's too late. I saw. I am not only a Mormon, I am a mystic. I am a romantic, transcendental, idealistic Mormon *mystic*." I converse with the Lord as one person would converse with another. And upon His invitation, I have recorded what He has taught me. And what I record is only a tithe of what He actually shares with me. And from that tithe I have only tithed again to produce the fraction I have shared with others. In this sharing with others, however, I find my nearness to the Lord has been magnified a thousand-fold. I have joy and rejoicing in serving as a labor assistant to those who are giving birth to Him in their lives; who are becoming thus born again, His sons and His daughters. And that rejoicing tells me I have found my way to the fulfillment of the measure of my creation. It tells me I have found my way to what I am, which is exactly what God would have me be.

---

[1]Ezra Taft Benson, "Born of God," *Ensign*, July, 1989, 5. (Emphasis added.)
[2]Madeleine L'Engle, *A Wrinkle in Time*. (New York: Doubleday, 1973.)
3Julia Cameron, *The Right to Write* (New York: J.P. Tarcher, 1999), p.3
[4]Ibid.

Wings!

Wings! Wings!
Dear God,
Give me wings.
What?
You already did?
Where?

There.
On your back.
Between your shoulders,
Folded up beneath
The burdens
You won't give to me.

An Imperative Duty

D&C 123

I went to the movies last week. I saw how Jo March did it. She took out her pen and her inkwell and sat down at a table in front of a window and wrote,…and wrote,…and wrote. And when she was finished she tied the bundle of hand-written pages up with a ribbon and sent them to a publisher and didn't get one rejection slip. She wrote a story about a girl writing a story about a girl.

Maybe I can do that. Maybe I can write a story about a girl writing a story about… No, at forty-six, I'd have to write about a woman writing about a woman.

I turn my back on my computer. It doesn't seem to mind. It calls up a screen saver to occupy itself. I pick up the mechanical pencil I just did nearly eight hours of editing with and reach for one of the three-ring binders I keep class notes in.

I pull my office chair off the hard plastic rug-protector, roll it across the carpet, and seat myself at my art table—the one I haven't spilled a drip of watercolor on in five years. I look down at all the familiar, years-old stains. I could probably scrub them off with some sort of abrasive cleanser, but then I might forget that I was once brave enough to work in watercolor—an art form not for the timid. Someday I'm going to have to paint again. I need to do that.

I take a dozen sheets of "college ruled" paper out of the binder, tap their bottom edge on the art table, and begin to write about a woman writing. One page flows out, without a single agonizing pause, and I see it's true: I needed a persona in order to write.

Why?

I don't know for sure.

Maybe because the real me is shattered, scattered. The truth is I can't guarantee that the next time I move, every cell won't fly apart and finally go its own solitary way.

Why?

I would guess it's because ever since there were two cells of me, I've felt it was two too many.

A strange thing to write?

Not for someone who is the product of a failed abortion, whose blood was alcohol-filled from before she had arteries of her own. Not for someone who was conceived not in love, but in need—a cellular deep need that flows through her veins even now, always burning—sometimes just stinging, but always there. *Always.* The need was there long before the blood, murmuring behind the walls of her mother's womb.

My son, Matt, comes in to visit with me. He's just home from school. Eighth grade.

"Mom, the scale in the front bathroom's busted. I don't weigh 118 pounds."

I look over my shoulder at him, quizzically. I have to agree with him. After all, he stands 5'10" and wears "extra large" everything.

"Are you sure?" I tease. Then I let my voice get serious. "You *are* looking thinner."

I mean it. He is. He's always been a chunky child. Not quite roly-poly, but soft and round. Now, he's beginning to lose his "baby" belly. His arms and legs are taking on contours as muscles enlarge, consuming the surrounding fat as they grow. His face is getting thinner, too. It's still smooth, though, and rosy. I don't tell him that. I don't think he'd like it. Actually, his entire countenance possesses a warm glow beneath his olive tan—with or without sun. And it all matches perfectly with his hershey eyes and his darkening hair. His hair was blond when he was six. But that was eight years ago. Eight.

He doesn't know my thoughts, or my searing need. For him, my talk is as healthy, as warm as his complexion; as hopeful as the little boy still so near the surface of his eyes.

He smiles at my comment about him getting thinner. "Really?"

He basks in the compliment for a minute, savoring his possible manhood and then retreats into the safety of childhood. He pats his tummy through his tee-shirt, slapping Garfield right where it hurts.

"Naw. It's just 'cause I untucked my shirt."

I notice he stands a little straighter, even so. He turns to leave my room.

"Love ya, Matt," I say after him, turning back to my writing.

"Me too." He returns what has become our traditional reply to expressions of love. It means, "I love you, too." It began when Julia, my youngest child, would say "me" in place of "I."

"Me wuv you," she would say and crawl up in my lap and give me butterfly kisses on my ears with her eyelashes. I'd squeal and pretend to hate it.

Alone again, I write about Matt's tummy; about Julia's eyelashes. She appears at my side. I didn't heard her come in. My bedroom's Grand Central Station nowadays—except when the need is raging, consuming me from within. Then I lie on my bed, hold a pillow against my heart to smother the need, and cry. At those times I close and lock the door and don't care what they watch on TV or how late they stay up.

"Mom, I'm going to the park. Okay?" She struggles to get her arm into her coat sleeve. Her hair, the color of the natural-oak headboard on my bed, falls in her face. She hates it when it does that. I know. She's told me a thousand times. She thought she'd like it long and permed—but she doesn't like to redeem the curls from the tangles every morning, unassisted. I listen to her fuss each morning, but I don't offer to help.

Gone are the days when my need pulled my daughters' hair to make them look good, to make them *be* good. It didn't work. Sunday mornings were the worst. The very worst. She doesn't know my thoughts or feel my need, either, thank God.

She bends over to kiss me with her lips—not with her eyelashes. The butterflies must be busy. She waits for me to turn full face to her. I forgot. Ears only work for butterflies. I turn and get a close up of her blue eyes that have turned sort of gray. That means she's bothered. I remember hearing her on the phone in the kitchen, a few minutes earlier, demanding that her best friend's little brother go call his sister to the phone.

"You are *not* Ilene," she had insisted. "You're Ethan. Ethan, go get Ilene!" Boys can be a pain when you're nine and they're seven.

She kisses me, lips to lips. By her hesitation she requires it. Sometimes cheeks, like ears, just aren't enough. But a fleeting peck, barely a touch, is.

She saw the movie with me last week. It had been a date. Just she and I. Girls' night out. First a chick-flick—*Little Women*—and then our favorite restaurant. A bean and cheese burrito a la carte and a Sprite with free refills. She always knows what she wants. Most of the waitresses do, too.

"See what I'm doing?" I take my stack of binder papers in both hands and tap them on the table top again, proudly displaying my top page filled with penciled script. "I'm doing what Jo did."

"You're writing to Joe?" she asks, thinking I mean her brother, Joel—whose name we often shortened to "Joe"; Joel—who's been three weeks in the MTC.

I'm not surprised she would think of him. It would take more than one movie to give the name "Joe" any other meaning. For a millisecond I remember her testimonies of over a year ago when her big brother was old enough for a mission but far from ready. Innocent of his shortfall, she'd walk up to the pulpit in fast and testimony meeting month after month, without any prompting, and say what was in her heart. No rote rhetoric from this family. One thing became routine, though: "And I'm thankful for my brother Joel going on a mission." Sitting in the back of the chapel, in the overflow, with all the other parents who had given up the fight to control their kids—whether nineteen months or nineteen years—I squirmed. I seriously doubted back then that Joel would ever be ready.

He was one of the children I had, in my own turn, conceived in need and not love. Like his siblings, I needed him to be good. To sit down. To shut up. To do his work. To go to bed. To go to school. To get good grades. To get his Eagle. To stay away from girls. To stay out of trouble.

It hadn't worked.

Need doesn't breed anything except more need. My life was certainly proof enough of that.

"No. No," I laugh at my youngest. "Not Joe." My intonation says, "Not *our* Joe." I hold the papers up and straighten them again, putting a little more dramatic flare in it. "You *know*. Jo." I lean on the rhyme between "know" and "Jo."

"Oh! Oh!" she exclaims. "*That* Jo!" You can tell she is pleased with remembering.

I'm pleased too. In fourth grade, she reads and writes nearly two grade levels behind. The resource teacher has tested her and she's been officially designated "learning disabled," though they can't pinpoint how or why. It's not your usual dyslexia or attention deficit disorder. Something more subtle, elusive, puzzling.

"Yeah. *That* Jo. I'm gonna' do like she did. I'm going to write and *write* until I have enough for a book, like her, and then I'm going to tie all the pages up with a ribbon and send them away to be published."

She turns to walk away, zipping her coat as she goes. I glance over my shoulder at her back. Her hair is puckered up between her neck and her coat collar. She reaches up and runs her hand under her hair, flipping it out of the collar. Without looking back, she says matter-of-factly, "And when it's a book, I will buy a copy and cherish it and read it to all of my children."

Seriously, she said "cherish."

"Love ya, Mom," she calls from the top of the split-entry stairs.

"Me too," I call back, but not loud enough. She's yelling something at me.

"If Ilene calls, tell her I'm at the park." I hear the front door close.

Two hours later I have four pages written. I've covered Matt's tummy and Julia's hair. Julia's kisses. Now it's quiet. I'm the only person in the house. Six bedrooms. Three bathrooms. And I remember the day when no one had a private bedroom, and hardly a private bath—especially not me.

Above the low electronic hum of my computer, I hear past voices echo off these walls. Actually, it's not exactly a hum the computer makes. It's more like the sound you can hear being communicated through the entire plumbing system when you've turned off the lights at night and in the near silence you realize you've left the water running in the backyard. I wonder what in the computer makes that sound, anyway? Something going around? A fan, maybe? That's probably it.

Scott, Joe's twin—Joe in the MTC, not Jo in the movie—is the computer whiz of our family. He told me once that computers get really hot and have to have a little fan running to keep them from melting down or blowing up or something. Scott wouldn't be going on a mission. His choices over the last two years had cinched that. Crap. Trying to picture the source of the noise inside the computer isn't keeping the memories at bay. Damn. That's about the most coherent thing I remember saying that day five years ago when my oldest daughter came home from exile to tell me something it had taken her five months of therapy to find the courage to say.

"Mom, are you home?" she called as she came up the front stairs.

"Damn." I whispered it under my breath. All I had to do was hear her voice and the turmoil started. The struggle between fear and rage welled up in my heart. I stared down at the towels on the bed in front of me and kept folding. It had promised to be a pretty peaceful Saturday. Early summer. All the kids were either outside playing or sleeping in. And then came Karen. Karen had blue eyes; at least that's what you thought at first glance. But then she stared at you, or you at her, and you realized there was a mother-lode of gold in her eyes, scattered around her irises like nuggets resting at the bottom of two sunlit pools. Unless she was mad. And then the gold seemed to shrink away. As if something stirred the gravel at the bottom of the pools and clouded the usual crystal clearness of her eyes. Believe me, no one, especially me, ever wanted to see that contrast between brightest sunlight and darkest shadow. Something inside me shrunk away in terror from the shadows in Karen's eyes.

"I'm in here," I called, not looking up from the laundry I was folding. There were at least four loads backed up on my bed. I hated folding clothes. Towels weren't so bad. I always did them first. But then there were shirts, jeans, underwear, socks. I hated it when work backed up.

Karen was my oldest daughter—my third child. She turned eighteen just days before she moved out, six months ago. I gave her an ultimatum: either quit staying out all weekend, using foul language around the house, and fold at least one load of laundry a day as a token effort to help the family, or get out.

She got out. Karen didn't do anything she didn't want to do. Not a thing. At least that's what I thought until I found her journals that late August Sunday when my second oldest daughter and I went to clear out Karen's tiny sixth of the student apartment she shared with five roommates. We gathered her things—her curling iron, her makeup, her toothpaste, her sanitary pads, her clothes, a few dishes, a towel or two. And then I found her journals in a box under her bed. I almost missed them. I picked one up, opened it and suddenly felt crushed by the same power that had held me up since the highway patrolman came to my door the night before. Now that same power sat me down to read.

> *I can't stop. I can't. What am I going to do? I was clean for three days and now tonight. Oh God. I think I've met my destroyer.*

But on that early summer morning of laundry folding, there was no clue we'd bury her in three months. No clue at all. Thank God. That morning had enough of a death knell to toll. I barely glanced up as she came to the doorway of my bedroom and leaned against the door sill.

"Where is everyone?" she asked. Her voice had that sound in it I dreaded; it meant she was tense, simmering inside, just waiting for someone to bump her right—which was exactly what I had a gift for—the ability to find her trigger. And if that wasn't enough, it was only a reflection in a mirror of how she affected me. Ten minutes or twenty-five words with Karen—whichever came first—and we were fighting.

It hadn't been that way when she was little. As a baby she'd been the answer to my prayers. I waited three babies to get my own little doll. And she was one. Tiny, tow-headed, she had a ready smile, with sparkling eyes, and double dimples on both cheeks. "Angel kisses," we called them, and I made sure they were never neglected.

But then something changed. As she grew older, tension formed between us. She was always what I called "feisty." A live wire. But by puberty that wire was one short fuse and I was at a loss to understand what was happening. By high school we were having full-fledged fights—mostly verbal, laced with stabbing words on both sides. By her eighteenth birthday, we had exchanged blows. Glancing blows, but blows nonetheless. I wonder if the bruises will ever heal without her here to exchange amends.

But that morning I was too defensive to consider amends. I was grateful for the relative peace I could sustain since she moved out. I was proud of her independence. After all, I lived alone when I was seventeen and a half. Of course, I hadn't had "good LDS parents" and a gaggle of brothers and sisters.

"They're all out playing," I volunteered, wondering if she felt guilty, watching me fold all these clothes alone—the chore she would rather desert her family than do.

"Where's Dad?" For a second I caught a different tone in her voice—sort of lisping, slurry. I looked up to see if her eyes were bloodshot. Sure enough, they were. Just as I thought. She'd hung one on last night. I turned my back on her and continued folding as I answered her. "He's up at Maple Dell, with Matt and Derek on a scout activity. What'd ya want Dad for?" To hit him up for money?

I didn't say the part about the money out loud. I just thought it. I look back now and I don't know why I had such a grudging, blaming attitude toward her about the subject. Handing out money was the only parental involvement his children ever received from him.

She didn't need to hear the words. She heard the tone, the tinge of sarcasm in what I said.

"It's not what you think, Mom." Her voice was taking on a tense, defensive edge already. I felt my jaw tighten up. The energy in the room was electric. The peace was gone. Damn.

I don't remember how it came to be that she entered my room; whether she walked in of her own accord before I began to rage at her, or whether I dragged her in after I lost it. All I remember is that within ten minutes I had her backed against the wall on the far side of the room, sobbing her eyes out as I yelled at her for her rotten and ungrateful attitude. I remember she had her hands up to her face and was trying to shout me down between her shaking fingers—trying to get a word in edgewise.

"You just don't understand! You just don't understand!" She kept repeating those words over and over, and with every repetition I got angrier.

"What in the h— do you mean? *I* don't understand," I ranted. How many times did I have to give her my "I-grew-up-in-the-slums-and-my-mother-was-a-whore" speech before she figured out how lucky she was to have me—a dedicated, selfless mother. Someone who cooked and canned and cleaned and crafted sixteen hours a day and slept *only* with her father the remaining eight. "You think you've seen something I haven't seen? You growing up in a decent LDS home, with a mother and a *father* to take care of you. You think you know something about this stinking world I don't know?" I challenged. "Then tell me what that might be! Go ahead, tell me."

Gasping for breath, trembling as if her bones were about to dissolve and she was going to crumple into a heap of dirtied laundry at my feet, she finally told me what she had seen that I hadn't. What she knew that I didn't.

"Mom,— Mom,— Mom,— ." She kept beginning and faltering. Something in her voice was different. New. No, old. She sounded like the little girl I'd known before the chasm opened up between us. She sounded like the little girl I had been before the chasm opened up in me to protect me from what no child should ever have to know.

I heard her voice echoing across that abyss, and like a bat, flying not by sight, but by sound, I could "see" the terror in its depths. Something in me wanted to run from the familiar choking sound of it. I knew too well the sound of her anguish, of her need. Need. Need. Need. It felt like the word was my pulse, pounding at the back of my hermetically sealed mind. My heart fled its quiet, unobtrusive place in my chest and was pounding instead in my stomach, at the back of my neck, in my hands.

"Mom,—" her voice failed her again.

Though my body didn't move, my soul cringed from the size of her eyes. Though logic would tell you no eyes could get that big or look that black, logic made no difference at a moment like this. Her eyes were huge, full of terror. No feistiness, no bravado, no distracting resemblance to sunlit pools and flashing gold. Her irises were tiny rings of light—like the corona of a hidden sun—behind her dilated pupils.

I saw myself,—my mother,—my grandmother who I have never even met,—all reflected there; generations of women who died, riveted through the heart with a tradition of their fathers—a lie that thrives in silence.

I knew before she spoke that no amount of being busy, no amount of pretending and denying was going to stop the truth from being spoken. Someone had convinced Karen she needed to tell.

Her voice had only the barest volume to it.

"Mom,—" She paused again. Now she wasn't gasping for breath. Instead, she seemed frozen in the middle of a breath, terrified of the words her lips were forming. Something inside me *knew* why she paused: she was sure that if she used this breath to tell this truth, she would never breathe again. I have often thought, since, of the little boy who gave blood to save his sister's life, convinced he would die from the act. Karen was about to risk her life for my sake. To kill the lie in me.

I listened as she told her story of being sexually abused. God, no. Not this. How could you do this, God? How could you let it happen to her? How could you let some heinous perpetrator do this? How could you let him infect her with his hideous emptiness, this groping, soul-murdering need?

I took her in my arms and she clung to me with all the terror she'd kept secret from me, trying so hard to follow my sterling example of longsuffering. I half carried her to the side of my bed, where we sat down together among the nice, neat folded piles of laundry and wept until we knew we were not dead.

♌

I've got to come up for air. I've spent years backing away from the day I would write this, and now it's one in the morning and I can't stop.

Derek just wandered down the hall to the bathroom and back to his bedroom. He has his favorite two fingers in his mouth and half of an old green basketball jersey clutched in his free hand, held close to his nose. It's silky. The jersey, not his nose. He's eleven, and the fingers and the "silky" are pretty much a thing of the night. A guard against the terrors.

"Hi, Mom," he mumbles as he stumbles past.

"Hi, babe," I answer, glancing up from my computer.

I found myself wishing he'd reappear at my door, as he had several hours ago, before he went to bed. I smiled at the memory. It was sweet. Thank God for sweet moments. Then he had been wearing his big sister's old ski goggles upside down and a toy army helmet on his head. In his hands he held—in battle ready position—a plastic, camouflage-colored, automatic machine gun. After a salute, which I returned, he informed me he was assigned to guard me from the enemy.

I didn't feel right telling him it was too late.

In My Gethsemane

When I came to
My Gethsemane,
Crushed,
Beaten.
On bloody hands
And knees.
Guess
Who I found
Waiting there for me.

Train Up A Child

Proverbs 22:6

It was August. Late August. It was late in the day, as well as the month. Later than I realized.

At 9:15 P.M., the sky was still light outside the open window above the bathtub. Have you noticed how the sun seems to cling to each day of summer? In winter it hurries across the sky as if embarrassed by its lukewarm weakness, shuttling quickly past in order to escape our sight. In summer, though, the sun rules the heavens and gives up to the night as reluctantly as the myriad of children that fill my secure Mormon neighborhood.

If fact, if it hadn't been a Saturday evening—the one evening of the week when every mother in every home on my street calls their kids in early to bathe in preparation for the Sabbath—I would have been alone in the house when the doorbell rang. I would have been sewing, or cleaning, or baking, or on the phone talking hope in Christ to a fellow mortal who, like myself, was struggling with the effects of addictive behavior in their own life or in the life of a loved one. As a lay counselor in an addiction recovery program, I have shared a lot of such support over the years and received tenfold as much as I have shared. Thank God. That night I would need it.

Since it was a Saturday evening, I wasn't alone in the house. In fact, all of my children under sixteen—eight of them to be exact—had finally come straggling in from "hide-n-seek" and "follow the judge to court" and were now watching a video, waiting for their turn in the tub.

Meanwhile, I was on my knees, my gut pressed against the side of a tub boiling with bubbles and bath water, trying to keep the shampoo out of my youngest child's eyes as I lathered her hair. Shiny and slithery with soap, Julia slid around in the six inches of water like a little eel, not cooperating at all.

Behind me, at the closed door, came yet another demanding knock. I fully expected to hear Derek's five-year-old lisping voice, insisting again that I open the locked door—never mind the four times I had already told him it wasn't his turn yet. In the background I could hear the familiar sound of a Disney refrain from *Mary Poppins*.

I was about to yell at him again, "Derek! Go watch TV. I told you already, we'll be done in a minute." Then I realized that this time it was my fourteen-year-old, Joel, knocking.

"Mom. You need to come. There's someone at the door that wants to talk to you. I think it's important."

"Ouch! Ouch!" Julia put her three-year-old, bubble covered fists up to her eyes, trying to rub the shampoo out of them.

"No! No!" In exasperation, and with a clobbering sense of fatigue, I raised my voice at her. Great. Whoever was on the front doorstep just below the open bathroom window was sure to have heard my tone of voice, my barely contained anger. What if it was someone from my ward?

Well, too bad. In defiance to whoever it was on my doorstep at such an ungodly hour on Saturday night, I made no attempt to hurry. Let them wait. Or better yet, go away. Calmly, I turned the tap on, adjusted the temperature and wrestled Julia onto her back. I did lower my voice, though.

"Lay back, babe. Relax. The water will wash the shampoo out of your eyes. Put your hands down. Stop struggling."

Still crying, she complied. The cries subsided to whimpers and I sat her up.

"Mom! Mom!" Now it was my ten-year-old's voice at the door. "You need to come to the door, Mom."

"I know. I know, Rachel. I'm coming as fast as I can."

I lifted Julia over the edge of the tub, stood her on the already half-saturated bath mat and started drying her hair.

"It's a policeman, Mom." Joel and Rachel's voices came through the door in unison. I could tell they were both standing outside the bathroom door with their faces pressed against it.

My heart sank through my stomach. "Oh, crap," I muttered. I draped the towel around Julia's shoulders and climbed to my feet. The knees of my jeans were wet.

A policeman. *Another* policeman.

The arrival of policemen at our house was becoming an all too frequent occurrence.

The first time was last fall when I made the decision to report Matt's bruises to the police. After all, his eight-year-old back and face were covered with them. The outline of his sister Karen's open fingers were raised in welts among the already bluing circles where her fists connected. While her dad and I were attending the temple that morning, she awakened with a hangover from the combination of alcohol and drugs she had used the night before, discovered three dollars missing from her dresser, and singled Matthew out as the culprit. However unsteady she was on her feet, she had enough coordination to find him, catch him, and pound him unmercifully.

Worse than the bruises on Matt's skin was the look in his eyes when I found him curled up on his bed, sobbing. All his life, he had adored Karen. He was her special baby brother. She was eleven when he was born. She voluntarily took care of him every afternoon for the first six months of his life. From the minute she came home from school until bedtime, she was within arm's reach of him, walking the floor with him, rocking him, kissing his little newborn face and whispering condolences over and over. "It's okay, Mattie. It's okay." A little fire-brand already at eleven, she was idealistic and super-achieving. School, soccer, Primary, housework, baby-tending. The oldest daughter, she excelled at it all. And I let her.

"It'll be otay, Mattie," she crooned baby talk to him. Apparently she convinced him. He settled in and began to thrive, even though he was the tenth child born into our family in twelve and a half years. I know he thrived, at least in part, because of Karen's constant attention. They developed an extraordinary bond that, in these last months, her addiction was swiftly destroying. He, more than any other sibling, was traumatized by her weekend-long disappearances followed by her fits of cruel sarcasm and rejection of the family.

Then came the morning of the missing money, the absent parents, and the cruel beating. For months I had begged her, told her, warned her I would not put up with any really serious trouble. So I called the police.

It wasn't been an easy decision. On our street, the appearance of a policeman was good for months of reminiscence and outright gossip. In the eight years we'd lived in this house, the only other time a policeman had stopped on our street was almost three years ago, the night the Bingham's son, Phillip, fell out of the tree where he was hiding during a summer night game of Ollie, Ollie, Oxen Free. He hit his head on a retaining wall and nearly died. His mother, Carol, was troubled by a feeling that "something was wrong," sending her from door to door searching for him. Soon scores of neighbors, members of our LDS ward, joined her, scouring the block with flashlights of all sizes and shapes. The doctors later said Phillip would have died if not for his mother's instinctive sense of trouble.

No such instinct troubled me this Saturday night.

Again it was Karen's behavior that brought the police to our home the second time. Several months after the day she had beaten Matt, I called the police to ask what to do with the bong-pipe I found under her mattress. I wasn't looking for trouble that day either. I had just finally given up waiting for Karen to change her sheets—a task she had neglected for weeks. The dispatcher said they would send an officer out to pick up the pipe and take a report. I had no idea when I called the police station that this was the standard procedure. I offered to bring it down to the police station. The young woman on the phone firmly refused my offer.

The officer arrived in his squad car within minutes of my call. I guess in Orem, Utah, police aren't as busy as they are in other places. Maybe he had been cruising by, making sure the latest snow was shoveled off the sidewalks.

The third time a policeman came to our door, was just four days ago. This time it wasn't about Karen. The doorbell rang about three in the afternoon. I stood there conversing with the tall, slim man in the dark blue uniform, badge and buckles, black leather belt and holster shining in the August sun. Herds of elementary school children were passing by, just coming home from year-round classes. Noisy and boisterous, glad to be out of hot classrooms, they often kicked off their shoes and started water fights as they meandered toward their respective homes. That particular day, however, they weren't bored enough to start fights. In fact, they were relatively subdued as they coagulated into little groups along the edge of my front lawn. Some were peering into the interior of the gleaming white police car, duly awed by its gold lettering; the bank of blue, red, and yellow lights fastened across its roof; and the caging separating the front seat from the back. My nearest neighbors' kids, made bold by years of shared family life, stood at the bottom of my front steps, side by side with my own grade-schoolers.

The officer was impatient, disapproving. He had come to tell me he was looking for my son, Matthew, who had taken off on another child's bike from the school grounds about twenty or thirty minutes ago. The parents of the other kid were enraged and demanding the police department find the thief. They found the bike just around the corner from the school, abandoned carefully on someone's lawn—no sign of Matt, but eyewitnesses had identified him positively. While there wouldn't be any charges pressed *this* time, if it happened again the parents wanted me to know they would do just that.

If it happened again? I was shocked at their reasoning. It wasn't like Matthew had a history of acting like this, of stealing anything from anyone, much less them exclusively. Why would they think he'd do it to them, *again*? Were three visits from the police in less than a year earning our entire family a reputation?

Matthew came home an hour later, sneaking in the downstairs basement door. He crept to his room and hid under his covers— just as he had the day of the beating.

And now, for the *fourth* time, there was a policeman waiting for me at my front door.

I unlocked the bathroom door and emerged into the hall, looking toward the TV room off the kitchen to see if Matt was there. He wasn't. I wondered if he was hiding again. I wondered if he had stolen another bike.

Or maybe it was Karen who was in trouble. Since she moved out six months ago, I hadn't had much contact with her. Even after the day when she came home to tell me about the sexual abuse she had suffered, the day we sat in the piles of clean towels on my bed and wept over the loss of her innocence and my ignorance, we hadn't seen much of each other. That was just a few weeks ago.

I held her that day and whispered to her, "It'll be all right, Karen. It'll be all right," in the same tone she had once used with baby Matthew. She clung to me and sobbed. If she had been any smaller I would have pulled her onto my lap and rocked her.

I turned the corner from the hallway to the top of the split-entry stairs and looked down at the two figures standing in the now-gathering gloom of my front doorway. The sun had given up its hold on the evening and finally admitted its need to be done. Where had it gone? Only moments before there had been that warm, pink alpine glow that characteristically casts across Utah Valley from the west, against the east mountains in the evening.

Though the light was totally gone, the August night air was still full of warmth. I could feel it battling with the air conditioning to get in through the open doorway. There were no lights on in the house. Julia, clad only in the towel, and all seven other children—Matthew wasn't hiding after all—were standing around me, or kneeling on the couch that backed against the black wrought-iron railing that separates the entry from the living room. They peered down over the back of the couch and the railing like the "peanut gallery" I often called them.

Both of our cats, usually relegated to the outdoors, had taken this opportunity to come indoors. Gingerly, probably surprised at having no children scoop them up to toss them out or maul them, they circled the men's legs then climbed the stairs. The glow and sound from the TV flowed around the corner into the living room and down the stairs at my feet.

I recognized one of the two men who stood on the step. The other was in uniform.

"Colleen?" It was my bishop's counselor, Karl Dunn, who spoke first.

I was confused. Relief that it wasn't some irate father accompanying the policeman clashed with bewilderment that Brother Dunn was there at all. My mind was searching desperately for some sense in what was happening. As I look back, it feels as if the events were already taking on a slow, surrealistic motion, as if some part of me knew what was coming and was trying to postpone it.

"Colleen," Karl began again without waiting for me to acknowledge him. That's the first moment I caught the urgency in his manner, in his voice. Time slowed down even further. It seemed to take me several minutes to descend the half dozen remaining stairs.

"Is your husband home, Colleen?" Something about his question stopped me on the bottom step. I still stood slightly above them. Some of my children trailed me down the stairs.

"No. He's out of town on a business trip. He'll be home in the morning."

"Wow! Look at all the badges!" one of the children hanging over the railing exclaimed. "How come you have so many badges?"

Hearing my child's question and then seeing the uncomfortable half-smile of the uniformed man standing beside Karl Dunn, I was suddenly aware of something else that did not compute. He wasn't dressed like any of the policemen I'd met before. He wasn't wearing a holster and gun, or a night stick. His uniform was brown, and it definitely was decorated with a lot of ribbons. He held a hat in his hand which he turned a couple of times before looking up. His gaze met mine and I caught a glimpse of something I didn't want to know.

"Colleen." It was Karl speaking again. Still trying to get through the thickness of the congealed time that was threatening, already, to grind to a complete halt.

"I'm sorry, Colleen. Since Gary isn't home, I'm afraid we'll have to talk with you."

Maybe Matt had stolen Karl's son's bike. No. His son was only four.

Maybe Matt had stolen *Karl's* bike.

Why was he here?

Why was he with a highway patrolman?

Utah Highway Patrol. The beehive emblem on the man's shoulder finally registered on me.

No. This wasn't about Matthew and stolen bikes. It had to be Karen. Maybe she'd been picked up for drug use. They had her in custody. I could handle that.

For the first time the highway patrolman spoke.

"Could I please have your full name?" he asked.

"Of course." I told him my full name.

"Mrs. Bowman, I need to confirm that you are the mother of Karen June Bowman?"

"I am."

Maybe they had her for possession…trafficking?

Maybe she had been in an accident.

Maybe she was in the hospital.

In a millisecond, I was in each one of those projected scenarios—talking to her across a desk at the police station; sitting by her hospital bed, holding her hand; waiting outside ICU; bringing her home in a wheelchair…

"Mrs. Bowman, I regret to inform you—"

There wasn't a sound in the house. Had someone turned off *Mary Poppins?*

"Just a spoon full of sugar makes the medicine go down—"

No. It was still playing away. Playing away.

"—that your daughter, Karen June Bowman,—"

His words were clipped, short, to the point, sharp, practiced, chosen—like the moves of a heart surgeon trying to cut only as deep as he absolutely had to.

"—was killed in an automobile accident on I-15 at approximately 5:15 this afternoon."

I don't remember what I did then, what I said, how I gestured with my hands or with my face. I don't remember with my conscious mind, but I know I heard some of the gasps that escaped several of my children.

"Karl," I heard someone say. "Please, hold me." I stumbled off the bottom step and Brother Dunn put his arms around me. I felt mildly surprised that he could see or hear me. I stared over his shoulder at the stars beginning to appear in the evening sky. My soul felt like a computer on search, scanning the entire universe. Where was she? Where was my child? She wasn't gone. She couldn't be. She had to be somewhere under those same stars.

It would have been one thing had it been a grandparent or a friend who died without my knowing it for all of these hours, but my daughter? I couldn't comprehend that for over four hours now, I had been in the world, while she was not. I had gone on breathing, eating, talking, laughing, worrying over bills.

Shouldn't a pit have formed in my stomach four hours ago? Shouldn't I have felt at least a twinge of nausea as she died? Shouldn't it have felt like someone was peeling away a piece of my soul? Shouldn't a shiver have gone down my spine as she passed? You know, like they show in the movies. I mean, even Lassie has more sensitivity, more intuition. I mean she *knows* when there's even a quiver in the fabric of her loved ones' lives.

But not me. No, not me.

The front of my wet shirt, the knees of my wet jeans, suddenly chilled me.

Numb, I looked from the stars to the porch lights. Every porch light on my street was on, and more lights were moving toward me. Cars came from every direction, parking up and down both sides of my street. Figures walked toward me in the dark. Neighbors. Ward members. Carrying flashlights. Maybe they could help me find Karen, the way they helped Carol find Phillip that almost fateful night three years ago. Or maybe I could step out into the street and call Karen home: "Ollie, Ollie Oxen! All home free."

To My Third Child

Mindful of you, the shining slopes this year,
And all the snowflakes that will this season fall;
Drift down, expecting to hear you call
"It's snowing! It's snowing!"
And see you fear
Not being the first
To turn them to a tear
On your warm, inviting tongue.
But all,
All wait in vain,
And instead create a pall
Across your grave,
Not on a slope, but near,
Where you were wont to go
On flying skis—
Rejoicing,
Flashing,
Shining,
Loving snow.
It misses you and whispers to me,
Please,
To somehow,
O God,
Somehow let her know.

Flight from Fear

But they that wait upon the Lord shall renew their strength; they shall mount up with wings as eagles. (Isaiah 40:31)

I'm in seat 16-A. I was supposed to be in seat 16-F, but a lady wanted to sit on that side of the plane—the side with three seats—so she could sit with her two small children. I had a friend, once, who changed seats with her sister during an automobile journey from Provo to Las Vegas and lived to tell about the accident that took out her sister's side of the car. My friend spent a lifetime in agony, unable to forgive herself for not being the one who died. I know I'd have a hard time forgiving myself if the mother and her two children died instead of me. Then again, I'd probably have an equally hard time forgiving myself if I died. Besides, this train of thought is a little superfluous, since I'm on a plane. If the plane crashes, we'll most likely all die. Comforting.

I can't believe I didn't bring a single thing to read. I did bring a half-empty note pad and a pen or two. That should stand me in good stead. Two and a half hours to do nothing but write. Two and a half hours from Salt Lake City to Minneapolis, Minnesota. And then a short hour and a half hop to Detroit, Michigan. If I were back home at my desk in Orem with four full hours of uninterrupted time to write I would think I'd died and gone to heaven. Hmmm, there I go again. "Flying doesn't have to mean dying." Maybe if I write that three hundred times.

The plane's moving away from the terminal. It's turning and taxiing into position for takeoff. It jolts and creaks as it hits bumps in the concrete. I notice the molding that covers the seam in the cabin interior just inches from my face is missing some screws and flopping up and down with each jolt. No, let's not exaggerate. It's just wiggling, not flopping. I look out at the wing, at the different panels of metal, held together by rows of rivets. I wonder if the rivets can come loose. Then I notice the panels are different colors. Not colors, really. Different degrees of shininess in the sun. Does that mean some of them have been defective at some point and had to be replaced? My heck, the wing's a quilt!

The plane makes a full 180 degree turn and sits still, shuddering with a sense of pent-up power I can hear, but not with my auditory nerves. It is a sound that I feel in my bones, drowning out the roar of the huge engines only feet from where I sit. It isn't something I perceive with my conscious mind. The truth is, my conscious mind is on the verge of overload trying to fend off memories of all the airplane tragedies I've read about. I hear this hum in my unconscious mind—the sound of molecules colliding with each other, the sound of a terrifying amount of energy, trembling to be released. I picture the plane crouching at the head of the runway, staring straight ahead, like my cat, Squat, when he's gathering his every muscle for the pounce and the kill. He was always bringing home dead birds. I certainly hope there'll be no kill today. No earth-bound pounce. Only free, faultless flight. But what if?

Come on, I tell myself. What if *what*? After all, *thousands* upon *thousands* of people fly every day. Yeah, but I bet all those others are not as terrified as I am. What if my terror gives off enough energy to interfere with the plane's electronic guidance system? I picture the explosion upon impact and the pages of this note pad miraculously unharmed, found among the debris scattered across the crash site. *Really*. Do other people on airplanes think like this?

The engines roar. The plane begins to move forward. With ever-increasing speed. Forward. Forward. Still forward. Rumbling. Terrific sound. We're still earthbound. We're racing toward a twelve-foot chain-link fence and the westbound lanes of I-215 at nearly 200 miles per hour.

And then up! The plane leaps into the sky at a forty-five degree angle. Instantly I feel like I've lost the fifty pounds I gained during the acceleration, plus fifty more. My insides feel suspended. The chain-link fence is twenty stories below the belly of the jet by the time we reach it. By the time we pass over, the cars on I-215 are the size of the cars in the board game, *Life*.

Wow! I forced myself to keep my eyes open that time, not like all the other times I've flown—seven times in forty-seven years.

I don't remember the first time I flew. It was in 1951 and I was almost three. We flew on a DC-10. Overseas to Paris. My father had a government contract to build runways in Algiers. He was a natural for the job, having served in North Africa in WWII. My mother and I flew over, alone, to join him in Algiers for the last three months of his stay. We took a boat home. I don't remember that trip either.

The other six flights were after my marriage. On every one, I closed my eyes at the first sense of forward movement during take-off, personally lifting the plane into the sky by my very own armrests, and hardly relaxing my grip until everyone else in the cabin was on their feet, pulling carry-on bags out of the overhead bins, speaking in hushed tones and shuffling out of the plane.

Fortunately for me, four of those six flights were only an hour long. It took my shoulder muscles only a day or two to unknot each time. The flights to and from the Micronesian island of Guam, however, took weeks to recover from. Fourteen hours in the air, each way, with an hour layover in Hawaii. By this time in my life, I was a wife following her husband on an assignment for the Federal Government. Unlike my mother who had only one child to fly with, I had eight, and the oldest was ten. I had too much to do to worry about whether the plane crashed. Just managing three meals in flight, continual trips to the tiny restroom, and changing diapers on my three youngest—a set of twins and another baby thirteen months apart—was enough to distract me from thoughts of death. And I was four months pregnant, *again*. Come to think of it, I might have looked upon a crash as a reprieve.

Today I am flying alone. No babies. No husband. In fact, the seat next to me is empty—at least of any physical presence. Being of a "mystical" mind-set, thinking like that is automatic to me. No babies. No husband. Those words summarize my life at this moment—on the ground or in the air. In the five years since my divorce, all my babies have gone away into adulthood or at least grade school. Now it's my children who are having babies. Three so far and three more this fall. In the face of the uncontrollable march of life, I will my hands to lie limp in my lap and try to leave my fate up to the laws of physics and God.

The plane is rocking back and forth. First one wing is up, then dipping down while the other tilts up. The horizon disappears out of my window and there is only blue sky. I remember the scene from *Apollo 13* in which the crew tries to keep Earth in the window in order to keep their bearings. I feel for them. I look up the aisle. We are climbing. Climbing. My ears are popping. I probably look like a seasoned flyer, calmly writing again in my note pad. "Flying is not dying. Flying is not dying. Flying is not dying."

Even though I'm all too aware that millions of dollars worth of technology and the amount of sleep the pilot got last night are really the deciding factors in my safe arrival in Minneapolis, I pretend my willpower adds something to the plane's ability to stay in the air. There is a dropping sensation—only a small one, like a ride at an amusement park. I'm not amused.

The bumpiness continues, increases. The bumps are really not any worse than hitting potholes on an old dirt road. I pretend I'm in a bus on a dirt road. Certainly I wouldn't think the bumps were going to rip the bus apart. Surely someone built this plane to handle a few bumps. I watch the rivets on the wings carefully. I sincerely hope someone has taken it upon him or herself to watch the other wing.

After my scrutiny of the wing becomes boring enough that death seems a viable alternative, I take a chance and glance down toward the ground. I glimpse the tiny ribbon that is I-15, laid north and south along the Wasatch Front. Suddenly snowy mountaintops are in my face. I can count the trees. We aren't any farther above them than we were above I-215 just after takeoff. The mountains are reaching for the plane, chasing it into the sky, pursuing it, trying to suck it back to earth with the pull of gravity. The left wing dips, and all I see is snow and trees. I hold my breath. Does the pilot know how close the trees are? This is no place to make a turn. Maybe he's asleep up there. I look over at the man in the seat across the aisle and a row ahead of mine. He is sleeping. Already?

We've left the Wasatch behind. Below us are ripples of snow-covered mountains running east and west. Their regularity is hypnotizing. I get the sense of the earth being a very slow liquid, like glass, forming waves over eons of time. Now we are leaving the mountains behind. The land below is flat and then flatter. Is this Wyoming? I remember driving across Wyoming once, at night. I didn't make it all the way. Its flatness got me then, too, and I gave in to my boredom and fatigue. I crashed at a Motel 8.

The sound of the plane's engines changes, like someone's shifting gears. I wait to hear them sputter or cut out. The sound changes again. What does it mean? I am tempted to be frantic to know, as if knowing would control it. Then sanity returns, and I have to smile at myself for thinking that my knowing would make even the slightest difference in the world.

A few minutes pass without us dropping out of the sky, and I entertain other possibilities for the change in sound. I notice there is less pressure against my skin, in my cells. There's more of a floating feeling. A voice over the loudspeaker announces we have reached our assigned altitude and will be cruising at 30,000 feet until we begin our descent into Minneapolis. Hmmm. Cruising? That sounds too easy. I'm not sure I like this floating feeling. I think I prefer the feeling of thrust, of pressure, of climbing—that makes me feel secure. It should take a lot of hard work to stay up this high.

After we were in Guam a week or two and had lived through a half-dozen small earthquakes, my former husband told me what I had not known before we moved there—Guam is atop one of the tallest "mountains" on the surface of the earth. It is approximately *six* miles to the bottom of the ocean not far off the island's coast. I was terrorized by that information. *Six miles!* What if one of these quakes didn't just shake the couch and rattle the dishes? What if it was a big one and we ended up buried in the depths of the sea? Considering the scriptural precedent set and the blatant presence of prostitutes in the hotel we were temporarily living in, frankly I was terrified. I mean, if God wanted to take out the wicked on the island of Guam, it's not a very big target.

Then my engineer-husband sated all my fears with a bit of wisdom that only an engineer could appreciate: "What difference would it make whether you were six inches underwater or six miles—you're just as drowned." I tried to take solace in a similar thought now, six miles in the air. Whether you fall from six stories or six miles, you're just as dead. Somehow, it didn't give me any comfort. It was the fall that petrified me—the several minutes it would take between knowing you were going to die and actually dying.

Determined to face down my fear, I force myself to stare at the nothingness six inches ahead of the wing's edge. I've read about aerodynamics, about how the curved upper surface of the wings causes the air to move faster over them, creating a lower air pressure. The air below rushes to fill in the area of lower pressure, and *up* go the wings and anything attached to them—like me. Still, how could the nothingness of empty air be filled with this power, this force, this "magic" that creates this impossible experience? And even more puzzling to me is how humans, able to manipulate invisible forces to achieve these kinds of miraculous results, can still doubt the presence of an organizing, managing Deity. Mankind aside, I was convinced and re-convinced. Flying puts me in touch with the incomprehensible.

I remember the hawk I watched in the mountains one day several summers ago, soaring effortlessly on the thermals, riding them in spiraling circles without flapping a wing. Any movement of muscle or sinew was so minimal as to be non-existent. The hawk banked left, caught an upward current and rode it as effortlessly as I ride an elevator.

"Look!" I exclaimed to a friend. "He's riding the winds of God." As I continue staring through the invisible air ahead of the wing, I realize I'm doing the very same thing—riding the winds of God. I am upheld and sustained by His Spirit—*Nephesh,* in Hebrew, means both "wind" and "Spirit"—looking down upon the Earth from a perspective He has inspired mankind to find their way to; a perspective He graciously shares. I think of Nephi and John and their "mountaintop" experiences (1 Nephi 11:1; Revelations 21:10).

"Let me trust Thee, dear God."

I almost forget myself and pray aloud as well as on paper. I lay my pen down, put my head back against my seat, close my eyes—

this time not in terror. I let myself become aware of my breathing. *Nephesh* also means "breath" in Hebrew. Breath, wind, Spirit. The connections weave around each other in my mind and heart. I feel that peace which "passeth understanding" (Philippians 4:7)—that makes no logical sense under the circumstances—beginning to affect my entire body. I find my whole "self" relaxing, entering a state of rest (Moroni 7:3) I have become intimately familiar with in these last eight years. It was with me at Karen's closed casket viewing, at her funeral, in the divorce court, during the lonely nights as a single parent with eight dependent children. It was with me through five years of college classes, as I have struggled to "fulfill the measure of [my] creation" (D&C 88:19) in ways I have felt as called to do as I did to my motherhood. I smile at myself for not realizing I would find that same peace here, cruising at 30,000 feet.

I undo my seatbelt, put my seat back and surrender totally to the truth of where I am. I let the Spirit of Truth flow through me as the wind flows over the wing of the plane. I am lifted to an even higher perspective. Without fear I let the truth sink into my soul. I am as suspended between life and death—between this world and the next—on the ground as I am six miles in the air. I can't be any more secure in my own respiration or pulse than I am the pulsing of the great engines. Facing that fact, rather than ignoring it, I am introduced into a consciousness of truth even deeper. I reconnect with the subliminal sense of power I felt while the plane was still on the ground. This time, though, I realize why the perception is only marginally connected to the sound of the engines. While this power is in the energy of combustion, so concentrated and harnessed in those engines, it is more. It is the power of aerodynamic principles and *more*. It is the power of wind and breath and *more*.

I can't control the little jerk of my diaphragm, the little breath out my nose that happens almost involuntarily when something humorous dawns on me. People are always saying it's no more dangerous to fly than to drive. I see now, it's true, as far as it goes. It just doesn't go far enough. The truth, the whole truth and nothing but the truth, so help me God, is that it's no safer to *breathe* than to fly. And you know, when you *really* think about it, maybe breathing is flying. Maybe taking that first mortal breath is leaping off the edge of somewhere long forgotten in the thrill of free flight.

Caught up in an energy that takes me to heights this plane could never reach, I am given the courage to examine other fears that I am flying from at this same moment in my life. The main one is the fear of establishing an intimate, possibly even marital, relationship with another man. I was kissed and I kissed someone for the first time in five years last night. I was flying as high then as I am now. I was as suspended between life and death, safety and tragedy, then as I am in this plane. Flying is a major risk; it's true. But so is living. From where I sit, I can't see any difference.

I'm relaxed. I think I might sleep, but I don't. Who wants to sleep and waste the chance to experience this miracle? I put my chair back upright and look past the wing and the rivets and the wind. I lean the side of my forehead against the window. Tears well up in my eyes as I gaze down upon the precious Earth, filled with love now my fear is gone. In the past I was never able to more than glance at the fact that I was so high. Now I am enthralled by the very same fact. I can see the sensuous, feminine curve of the horizon and I reflect on the expression "Mother Earth."

The Intermountain West is far behind. The terrain we're flying over now is not mottled with white, but olive drab, khaki brown splattered with scores and scores of tiny navy blue spots. Lakes? Maybe that's where all the white went, into navy blue low spots. It is fascinating to think the air, the sun, the pale blue horizon deepening to cobalt blue looks exactly the same here as it did over Utah—and yet it isn't the same. In the two hours that have passed, we have traveled north as well as east, turning the globe diagonally beneath us.

I notice some of the larger lakes have patches of white floating in their center. Child of the West—the desert West, to be exact—I have never seen ice form over large bodies of water. A scrap of textbook knowledge comes back and reminds me that ice will stay longer over deep water and melt more quickly over shallow. The lakes become larger. Many of them are ice covered, even though there is no sign of snow on the drab land between them. I marvel. With all this water, the land must be a plush carpet of green in the right season. It couldn't be any other way. I realize I must be looking at miles and miles of hardwood, deciduous woods. In early March it doesn't look any different than the sagebrush covering Wyoming.

Nevertheless, this is Minnesota. The land of 10,000 lakes. They are everywhere. There is no way a person can walk away from them; walk away from water. There's a lake within wandering distance of a child in any direction. The folks here must have to teach their children to swim before they can walk.

I look at my watch. If we are still on schedule we have less than half an hour to go. As if on cue with my thoughts, the sound of the engines changes once more. I look out the window. I don't notice much change in the size of things on the ground. Our descent is gradual. Clouds appear like scattered cotton balls. Another few minutes pass and the cotton balls below us crowd together, looking like the backs of fluffy sheep. I remember the pilot's prediction for Minneapolis—"partly cloudy."

I expect we will experience some more bumps passing through those clouds.

"Ladies and gentlemen, we are about ninety miles outside of Minneapolis. We have just been cleared for landing. In a few minutes we will begin our approach. If you are continuing on in your travels today, please listen carefully to the following connections."

I listen carefully. "Passengers continuing on to Detroit, Michigan, please go to Gate 31 on the red concourse." That's me.

I feel a sensation of increasing weight as the plane begins its descent in earnest. I look out at the land below. Minneapolis, Minnesota is my father's birthplace—the soil from which he grew, only one generation removed from his grandparents, immigrants from Ireland and Norway. Some part of the molecules in *this* land are in my body. I feel a very elemental attachment. I look out at the horizon, not blue any longer, but lavender. Pretty, but I suspect it's a result of the smog over the city. We continue to lose altitude.

I stay conscious for the landing this time; I do not retreat into clenched fists, closed eyes, and lowered brows. I keep writing. I remember reading somewhere that nothing—not even *moving* pictures—can capture an experience in the same way as the written word. Pictures, no matter how exquisite, can't take you inside the experience—can't tell you how it *feels* to *be* in the experience. That's what I want to capture as a writer. What it *feels* like to *be* in my life's circumstances.

The engines cut back—*way* back. It feels like they've been turned off, like we're gliding. The sound and the motion ebb to what feels like a stop. That's impossible. We can't stop in mid-air. We have to be moving forward. We must be. That's a principle of flight. Thrust creates lift. Gravity creates drag.

The wing on my side takes a deep dip. I look down at freeways, defoliated trees, a ball diamond. Then the wings level. There's another change in the sound of the engines. The nose is elevated.

The right wing dips slightly. Corrects. The left wing dips. Comes level. There is an increased sense of dropping. Down, down like I'm in an elevator.

There are trains, railroads, everywhere below.

I hear the landing gear go down—Ca thunk! The ride becomes bumpier as the air rushes into the open places in the plane's underbelly, as it flows around the giant tires.

We jerk and jump around as if we are on a very rough road.

We must be cutting more and more sharply through layers of air. I wait for that last straightening out to come, for there to be no more tilting and bumping. I am hanging on to the end, but I have to admit my eyes are closed now. I'm still afraid to watch the ground come up to meet us. As if my watching or not watching will make any difference in the end. Life will happen whether I watch or not—and watching, I might actually learn from what I live through. How easy it is to forget the truth when we're afraid.

I open my eyes. We are only ten stories from the ground.

Five, four, three, two, one.

The wheels hit, then hit again. We are on the ground. The engines reverse. I slide forward in my seat.

Forty miles per hour. Thirty. Twenty.

We turn and taxi slowly toward the terminal.

It's six minutes before we come to a complete halt. Passengers leap to their feet, crowding the aisle, pulling their belongings from overhead bins. Their faces are somber and weary, some glum and frowning. They are anxious—anxious to leave the plane, anxious to return to Earth. I press my face against the window one last time and look up toward the heavens, missing them already. A profound peace encircles me.

"Thank you, Lord," I whisper. "Thank you for counseling me, healing me."

In my notebook, I record His sweet response, "—as on eagle's wings, dear friend, as on eagle's wings."

From Generation to Generation

And the Lord God hath scourged them...for the space of many generations, yea, even down from generation to generation until they shall be persuaded to believe in Christ. (2 Nephi 25:16)

"Hello?"

I marvel at the pleasantness with which I can wake up, even in the middle of the night. The phone can ring once and if it's by my bed, I answer it out of a dead sleep with a warm, present, "Hello." I sound like I've been sitting up just waiting for the call.

"Hi, Mom, this is Merry."

I switch on my bedside light. I have to reach for it at an awkward angle. It's a tall, metal pole lamp, positioned between the edge of my bed and the edge of my desk less than a foot a way. Since my divorce three years ago and my return to full-time school as well as full-time writing and editing, I no longer have a desk in my bedroom. I have a bed in my office.

"Oh, hi, babe." I'm speaking to my second daughter—my oldest daughter now, since her sister Karen's death. I still can't comprehend that Merry is, at twenty-one, three years older than Karen, who will always be eighteen and nothing more.

"Are you writing, Mom?" I glance at my wristwatch lying on the headboard of my bed. Three in the morning. I don't own an alarm clock—I don't need one. I've never been able to get my mind to stay still long enough to need one. Five hours of sleep is the most my body will handle; some biological clock has it timed almost to the minute. To bed at ten, up at three. To bed at eleven, up at four. To bed at midnight, up at five. You get the idea. To be up at three A.M. writing or studying was routine for me. And my children—including Merry on the other end of the chilly phone— know it.

"No. No. I gave up the chase at midnight."

Merry left for work at ten the night before, grumbling about being stuck with another graveyard shift at the Conoco around the corner from our house. Apparently, she believed me when I'd half-heartedly told her as she left that I'd be up all night doing homework.

Doing homework during the day isn't possible for a single parent of twelve—even if half of them are grown and out of the home. But I don't do the all-night thing so well anymore, either. Not like I did during the sixteen years between my first baby and my last. While admittedly only a pittance, the five hours of sleep my body afforded me was absolutely essential to keep me functioning. The lack of any variation reminded me of my cheap laptop that gave me two minutes warning between full power and "hibernation mode," when the screen blacks out and the CPU's fan whines audibly as it keeps the processor cool.

I sit up on the side of the bed. Crumpled sheets of paper rustle around my feet.

I spent most of the prior day editing—rewriting, really—a journal article by a professor on "Fiscal Policy in Small Rural Hospitals." It—the rewriting part—hadn't come easy and still isn't finished. Then I realize my creative writing assignment isn't finished either. I wasn't sure whether writing about fiscal policy and rural hospitals had used up the muse in my heart or scared it away. I certainly felt I had nothing "creative" left; it was all on the wadded papers around my feet, giant popped-corn kernels salted with my vain attempts at sorting out rural doctors and their fiscal responsibilities.

"How are you doing, babe?" I ask easily, lightly. Considering she's been "tending store" all night and it's only her fourth night on the job, she sounds amazingly chipper.

"I'm pretty good. This last couple of hours are so long, though." She draws out the "so" and the "ah" in "long" for emphasis.

"I bet." I rub the sleep from my eyes, sincerely trying to feel for her. My mind keeps wandering back to the two pages—not all of my efforts were crumpled up—of writing I salvaged yesterday. I climb out of bed and move to my chair, a slight groan escaping my lips. At forty-five, it isn't easy unfolding anymore. I grope with my big toe for the switch on the power strip under my desk. My hard drive beeps and blinks to life.

Merry's voice continues. "Scott just left. He came in again to visit. He hung out with me for awhile. I can count on him to show up for the free donuts at three."

Scott is Merry's younger brother, twenty years old.

I keep thinking about the rural hospitals, their financial policies, the writing I did yesterday. Or rather, didn't do. What if this morning is like yesterday? What if nothing happens? What if the two pages I wrote yesterday make no sense this morning?

What if I'm still at ground zero? What if today, instead of writing, I spend my day running? Running back to what twenty-three years of homemaking programmed me to do—errands, housework, laundry, phone calls. I couldn't walk into class this evening empty-handed. My professor is expecting both rural hospitals *and* my creative writing assignment. I have neither.

Merry is unaware my mind has wandered. "Yeah, Scott and I had a good talk," her voice continues. "Really good."

I'm tempted to make that little snort through my nose, the kind you make when something cracks you up. Somehow it seems crazy. Who knows how many Family Home Evening lessons I gave on communication to either a room of stony, silent faces or a boiling cauldron of quarreling children. I shake my head. Twenty-three years of Family Home Evening lessons and Personal Private Interviews (a Mormon mother's version of Personal Priesthood Interviews, conducted without the participation of the father) and my children find "good talk" with their siblings at three in the morning between selling cigarettes and coffee to other nocturnal types.

Hmmm. Merry and Scott had a good talk at three in the morning between checking ID to sell beer and cleaning out the hot-dog roaster. Maybe I could turn that into an essay, I think. Maybe I could contrast Scott and Merry's dark-of-night conversations with the scenes of their childhood confrontations.

"Yeah. Did you know today is Scott's little girl's birthday?"

Merry's words jerk my mind back.

"No. Merry, I didn't realize that." Has a year already passed since that day in the kitchen?

♋

I spent the entire morning in the kitchen trying to undo the damage a week of midterms had done to my Molly-Mormon Mother mentality, shreds of which are still holding on even after three straight years of college—spring, summer, fall and winter. Seven days of Cap'N Crunch, peanut butter and jelly sandwiches, Pizza Hut, bean-and-bacon soup and a constant supply of chocolate chip cookies produced by my ten-and twelve-year-olds (you learn to bake chocolate chip cookies in this family before you learn the "Articles of Faith") can leave a kitchen pretty thrashed.

I stood at the counter trying not to knock any of the dirty dishes, soup cans, or empty cereal boxes off as I struggled to fold the pizza boxes in half so they would fit in a "tall kitchen" size garbage bag without ripping holes in it and making it worthless. I hated how pizza boxes did that. I hated how they required their own special trip to the dumpster in the garage. I was determined they wouldn't this time.

"Hi, Mom."

"Hi, Scott." I spoke without looking up, caught as I was in the battle of the boxes. Instantly, though, I knew something wasn't right. There was no sound of his footsteps coming into the room. There was no expected next comment, no word play. Clever, joking word play was Scott's specialty. Reading three grades ahead of his age since kindergarten, he was never at a loss for something to say, no matter what the subject or circumstance. Now in the kitchen there was so much silence, for a millisecond I thought I might have imagined the words I thought I heard. Still lying on the boxes with my upper body, trying to break them in half, I looked up at him.

He stood just inside the dining room end of the kitchen. At six-foot-one, 185 pounds, he was what some might call a "hunk." His dark-blond hair was short, missionary-cut. His huge blue eyes were filled with tears. His cheeks were wet. His nose was red.

Something inside me cracked. The image of a nineteen-year-old Mormon boy standing in his mother's kitchen, crying, just wasn't right. He should be staring at me from a snapshot, standing next to his companion, his arm around a dripping wet convert or two—all of them dressed in white.

Instead Scott stood there in my kitchen, looking like someone had just shot him. You know that look that comes over Mel Gibson's face in *Hamlet*, when he turns to his friend and says, "I'm dead, Horatio. I'm dead."

It's the look I had on my face four years ago, when Karen came home sober enough to tell me she had been sexually abused in her childhood. It was the look I had on my face four months later, when the highway patrolman told me she had been killed in an accident. It was the look on Merry's face when she handed her baby over to its adoptive parents a couple of years ago. It's the look people get when they're compelled to face the truth and the truth feels as terminal as a massive heart-attack or stroke.

As soon as our eyes met Scott found his voice. "Mom, Laura had her baby two days ago."

I stood and let the pizza boxes begin to unfold.

Before I could say anything, Scott spoke again. His voice was barely audible. "No one called. They didn't call me." He repeated it over and over. "They said I could come to the hospital and see the baby before they sent her away, but they didn't call me."

For a moment my mind struggled to keep the truth at bay yet again. No! No! Midterms, single parenthood, five children under eighteen still to raise, this creepy-crawly kitchen, the pizza boxes, the price of wasted "tall kitchen" trash bags. Surely that was enough reality for one woman to deal with in a day!

Scott repeated each sentence two or three times, wringing out each word like an obsessive-compulsive person might wring their hands. "They told me I could see the baby, Mom. They didn't keep their word." I cringed away from the truth of who "they" were who had not kept their word. We had been told by authorities at the adoption agency, by Laura's parents, by Laura herself, that we could see the baby—just once, at the hospital, before the adoptive parents took her home to love and raise, forever.

"They what?" I repeated myself at least twice.

"They what?" I still couldn't believe my ears. Of course, the baby *was* Laura's child. But she was Scott's child, too.

We had come to a consensus the last time we met with Laura's family at the Social Services office. On that occasion, Scott read a three-page, single-spaced letter to Laura and her family, apologizing for what happened. He wept then, too, and expressed his willingness to accept her family's decision to put the baby up for adoption. He told them of his gratitude for treating him so well during the past year, while he and Laura dated. Towards the end of the letter, he could hardly read through his tears as he expressed his concern about Laura's safety during the pregnancy and the baby's safe birth. I wept as I listened. I felt the witness of the truth—Scott had the rudimentary beginnings of a genuine fatherly love. I ached that it had to emerge as a result of such hopeless circumstances.

The social worker and Laura's father nodded and assured Scott they understood. Laura's mother sat absolutely still, though her cheeks were moist with tears. Laura sat like a statue, staring straight ahead.

I left the pizza boxes unfolding on the counter and crossed the kitchen to reach for the phone. "What's the hospital's number?" I opened the drawer to get the phone book. "Better yet, I'll call Social Services—"

Scott's voice stopped me cold. "It's too late, Mom. They already sent the baby away. She's gone. Her parents picked her up the same day and took her home with them to New York or somewhere."

The same day! How could they do it all so quickly? Didn't it take a day or two to give away a baby for eternity?

ℴ

"Yep, a whole year." Merry is still talking to me on the phone. "And tomorrow will be two years since I gave Bear up." "Bear" was Merry's pet name for her own little girl.

I am too overwhelmed to come up with a proper reaction. "Oh really? Has it been that long?"

My tone is Sunday-School-polite, Relief-Society-reserved. A little prayer would be more appropriate. Something like, "Oh God. Merry. Has it been that long already?" After all, she is talking about her own flesh and blood. My own flesh and blood.

I guess one's psyche can only hold so much pain, and then the mind does something to cope. It shuts down. It creates another persona. A mask. A facade.

Merry's voice is as fake, as "fine" as mine. She takes her cues well. The old don't-feel, don't-talk rule is not dead in our house. "Well, I'd better get back to cleaning up. I still have to mop. I'll see you in a little while."

"Okay, kiddo. See ya, too."

I hang up the phone and put on my robe. Merry calls it my "Moses robe." I have to admit that with its solid turquoise color, broken only by a vertical band of black down the center front, set between two stripes of white, it does look a little biblical. I feel blessed to have my mind turned to Moses. After all, he was an adopted child, separated from his blood relations and look how significant his life turned out to be.

I turn on the computer and call up the two pages left over from yesterday. I read through the description of hospital finances. My mind wanders again as I feel the warmth from the heater vent on my feet under the desk.

ℒ

Last night was a 'Last Days' night, weatherwise—one that sets at least one Mormon in three to pondering and pontificating about the change of seasons predicted in the scriptures. Even though it's the first week in March, last night was so warm it could have been an early summer evening. People were wearing only shirt sleeves at nine.

This morning, the weather has made a reassuring retreat into normalcy; the sky is solid clouds, gray on gray. In the little snatch of distance angled between the roofs across the street, the bottom edge of an especially dark cloud is blurred against the lower portion of the dark mountains, like water color painted wet into wet. It was raining over on the east bench.

From the look of the sidewalks in front of the house across my street, it's rained here too. But it's either been a while since it stopped or it hadn't been much to begin with. The cement is only dark in splotches. Anywhere there is the slightest shelter from the sky—under the edge of parked cars, for instance—it's perfectly dry.

My feet, tucked under my art table, are bathed in a blast of warm, reassuring air. Forced air heat. It's such a luxury, protecting us from the gray and the wet. Set on an automatic timer, it kicks in just in time to keep us from the discomfort of the season's reality. Ever-vigilant for our sake. Taking care of us. Once in a while, the house will get chill before the heater realizes it. Then someone will crank the thermostat up. Obediently, the dumb machine comes on and stays on. Fifteen minutes later, someone else will yell, "My heck! Why's it so hot in here?" Their eyes open wide when they see the thermostat in the hall. "Who set it on 80?!"

No one ever answers.

My feet feel hot. I pull them away from the vent. It takes a lot of heat coming out of the floor to raise the temperature in the entire house a degree or two.

I can never figure out how my children survive under the sheet or blanket tents they make over the blasting vents on cold mornings. I hear the heater running but feel no heat and find, upon checking, that there is a corpse-like figure, completely shrouded, laying over every vent. If it is only a sheet they've dragged off their bed, it will be billowing and rippling like a hot-air balloon, beginning to fill.

When I find them like that, I seldom scold them. It reminds me too much of the early mornings my cousin and I spent huddled over a heater vent eating crackers we'd sneaked out of my aunt's kitchen.

$\mathcal{L}$

"No! No! Not those! *Those!*"

My cousin's voice would rise above a whisper, risking waking up the adults in the house and spoiling our early morning raid on the kitchen. She had to speak up, though, so I could hear her over the sound of the heater blowing hot air under her nightgown as she sat on the vent. Besides, she wanted me to come back with the right crackers. Not Saltines. Saltines were for lunch with soup, with an adult hovering around. Ritz were for sneaking in the morning and pirating away to your secret place under the hardwood dining table amidst a forest of quality-crafted wooden chair legs—no chrome plated cheap stuff like at my house—topped with a flurry of floral seat covers, coordinated with the curtains at my aunt's kitchen windows and the wallpaper on the walls.

"Now, get the cheese out of the refrigerator." Cindy, at seven, was a great slave driver. At four and a half, I was the perfect slave.

I opened the refrigerator twice my height, and stared in awe at the crammed interior. I didn't know it was possible to have so much food in your home. It wasn't right to keep so much food when others were going hungry, was it? Hungry. I knew the definition for that. Nothing to eat. Nothing clean to wear. Hungry.

But that was back at my house in Rio Linda, California, a little rural area on the northeast perimeter of Sacramento. For the moment, I was over the rainbow, down the rabbit's hole, through the looking glass. I was at my aunt and uncle's home in San Mateo, just outside of Oakland, California.

At four years old, I had no idea how many miles lay between my world and my cousin's, but I knew it might as well have been on another planet. A planet where, twice a year—in the summer and at Christmas—my dad and mom would pretend to belong. They would stop drinking and fighting long enough to spend a few days with his sister, Lorraine, her husband, Tom, and their two children, Allen and Cindy. My dad and mom would dress me—the child they conceived out of wedlock, the child that was proving a poor excuse for a marriage, the child that was absorbing all the blame for their hatred and shame for their misery—in newly purchased pajamas on the way out of Rio Linda.

"If it hadn't been for that d— brat, I'd have never married you, you filthy b—! How in the h— do I know she's even mine?! You're such a wh—!" My father's words to my mother weren't always civil.

At least I guess he was my father. I couldn't be any surer than he was. Equally drunk, my mother had her own version of how if it hadn't been for him, the s.o.b., and the d— pregnancy she'd have been on her own, too, footloose and fancy-free.

Of course, they never yelled at each other or at me when we made our pilgrimages into the normalcy of the world of Lorraine-Tom-Allen-and-Cindy, in the galaxy of San Mateo.

At my aunt and uncle's house, I would explore their home and pore over the photographs covering the walls—pictures of Lorraine and Tom's wedding, pictures of Cindy and Allen, both planned and treasured children.

Allen, at eleven, was seven years older than me. His bedroom looked like something out of *Leave It To Beaver*. Since he was eleven and I was only four, his room was off-limits to me for two reasons: I was a girl and I was a baby. He was convinced I could never be trusted to keep my four-year-old deprived hands off all his untouchable stuff—his models, sports equipment, scouting gear, Erector set, chemistry set, trophy for Little League, and clarinet—not to mention his brand new phonograph and growing collection of singles, saucer size 45's with huge holes in the middle. It was the all-around, all-American, upper-middle-class, pre-pubescent boy's room. His room was a portion of Never-Never Land and I had no permission to enter. Ever.

Cindy was different. When I came to visit, by default I had a temporary guest's pass into her world of pink and lace. After all, I was a girl and I had to sleep somewhere. She shared her full-sized, canopied, dust-ruffled bed with me. For those few precious nights, she and I would pick a dozen of her Little Golden Books from the hundreds on her book shelves and snuggle down between the fresh sheets to read—she in one of her dozen nightgowns and I in my new pajamas, which still bore telltale department store creases.

Back in my world, the clothes I played in all day worked fine, most nights, for putting myself to bed in. Being my parents' only child, it was easy for them to get lost in their own concerns and forget such things as nightgowns, baths, and bedtimes—or sometimes even to come home.

***

I hear the front door of my house open. It's Merry coming home from the Conoco. Her in-line skates make a moment's noise on the tile floor in the split entry. Ever since the weather turned warm she's been rollerblading the six blocks to work and back.

Knowing I'm awake by the lamplight in the window, she calls to me before going downstairs to her room, "Mom, I'm home!"

"Good, I'm glad!" I call back, pausing for a second over the sentence I just wrote about being an only child, easy to forget. Luckily, or maybe blessedly, I ended up having enough children that I can't forget them or their needs. They take turns reminding me.

I take a few minutes to scan the pages I've written. I need to take a shower. I can't believe how physical remembering is. Visceral.

I also need to clean the kitchen. Though I don't have midterms as a current excuse, I've done a great job finding reasons to resort to fast-food, carry-out, and TV dinners. It makes me glad to think I use my Stafford Loan money to feed my family a varied diet.

I need to take the half dozen calls backed up on my voice mail from yesterday.

Before I can reach for the phone, I hear a voice behind me. "Mom, can I get in bed with you?"

Merry stands in the doorway, her face red and wet, streaked with mascara. Strands of long dark brown hair have escaped the scrunchie at the back of her neck and are stuck to her wet cheeks. Her forest-green sweatshirt with green plaid letters spelling "BYU" across her chest is hidden behind the arm full of baby blankets and baby clothes she clutches to her heart.

This time I can't push away her pain, as I did on the phone earlier. It lies scattered across my bedroom in the form of little sleepers and tee-shirts she drops as she stumbles past me, shoved from behind by the memories that haunt her.

"Mom, she was my baby. My baby's gone. Oh God, Mom." Her voice is muffled by the covers she's pulled over her head.

I lie down next to her shaking form and pull the edge of the covers back so I can caress the crown of her head. I fix my eyes on the poster hanging on the wall across from the foot of my bed.

Starting at the top, set against a black background, is a rainbow of printed words. They begin with "And thou shalt call his name Jesus,..." in yellow, and end with "The Alpha and Omega" in royal purple. It is a list of names and terms for Christ. In the very center, in bold, plain, white, two words stand off the paper. "I AM."

Once again I remember why I'm a mother. I am a mother because I AM. Years ago, when my children were little and neighborhood snowball fights and four-letter words were our worst worries, I wrote an essay that taught me that truth about myself. Motherhood is my essence, my soul. No matter what my children do or need, I am committed to this calling.

Silently, I lay my cheek against my daughter's hair and begin to pray a mother's blessing upon her and upon her daughter—and upon my mother's daughter. I pray my daughter will know her sacrifice was an act of love, that rather than divide her baby's sanity into pieces with shame and blame as she and I had been divided by warring parents, she had given her up to be loved. I pray she will know we have made progress over our two generations. I pray silently that soon she will return to the peace that makes no sense, the peace that passeth understanding, the only peace that works in these kind of circumstances, the peace of Christ's Atonement, of being sealed to Him, as His sons and His daughters. My own tears form and fall into her hair, an adequate anointing.

Lost and Found

Dearest Savior,
Good Shepherd,
Lift me high
Above Thy head,
A sacrifice.
My willful heart
Now dead.
Then lay me
Across
Thy shoulders, tenderly.

Let the blood
Of the stripes
Thou didst bear for me
Soak my garments
Through and through,—
For Lord of Mercy,
Grace,
And Love,
I have no hope
But you.

God, Popeye and Me

I squirmed in my seat, changing position. The baby on my lap, in utero, kicked hard. Trying to favor my already bruised rib, I sat up straight, desperately struggling to ignore my discomfort; to stuff it back into my subconscious.

I glanced over at the sharply upturned faces of my three youngest children (I was outnumbered in choosing how close to the movie screen we would sit) and wished for a portion of their easily enthralled innocence, or, if not that, a seat a couple dozen rows back. I stared up at the huge, grainy images towering over my head and tried to surrender to the situation. Considering the story line of the movie—*Popeye*—it should have been easy for me to relapse into my own childhood and find some relief from the chronic sense of confusion invading my heart and mind the past year.

The baby within me squirmed and I squirmed again. It was a dance we did with each other. First he'd move. Then I'd move. I felt a contraction begin. My abdomen tightened. It could have been a basketball on my lap instead of a baby. For a moment, neither of us moved. Then it passed. Braxton-Hicks. Nothing imminent. My uterus was just working out, training for the big day still two weeks away. This being my tenth child, I knew the routine by heart. I never came early. Never. I stared at the screen and willed myself to concentrate on the movie.

Booming from of a strategically placed sound system—strategically placed if you're seated two dozen rows back—was a musical refrain I had originally heard in 1956 when my dad brought home our first television. Popeye was a mere cartoon then, black and white, on a small screen. But here, right before my eyes, thanks to the foolery of Robin Williams, Popeye danced in the flesh, complete with bulging forearms, anchor-shaped tattoos, and a corn cob pipe.

The baby inside moved again, but my own "inner-child" was numb, frozen. Somehow, in the intervening years since she had run home from school every afternoon to watch Popeye, he and I had traded places. Popeye had become a three dimensional, living soul while I had become the cartoon—a caricature of a Mormon woman—much more likely to show up in a Calvin Grundahl or Pat Bagley cartoon book than on the slick, shiny cover of *This People* magazine.

I could see the cartoon now, showing a very pregnant woman waddling from the dining table to the kitchen sink, carrying an armful of dirty dishes. On the kitchen counter sit opened cans of pork-and-beans. Scattered about the kitchen/dining room are several preschool children. One is flipping pork-and-beans off a spoon at the one-year-old in the high chair. Another is feeding his bowl of beans to the family dog. Sitting on the floor, another child tears pages out of a book plainly marked, *Book of Mormon Stories*. On the bulletin board above the table are various papers tacked up next to an oversized calendar. One of the papers says, "Don't forget your visiting teaching." Another is marked "PTA board meeting." The calendar says "Elder's Quorum Meeting, 7:00 P.M., TONIGHT." Hanging next to the bulletin board is a framed cross-stitch that says, "No Other Success Can Compensate for Failure in the Home." Taped to the cupboard next to the sink is a sign, "Mother sets the mood in the home." Standing in the doorway of the room, with a book bag marked "HOMEWORK" trailing behind him, is an older child asking, "Mom, when will Daddy be home from church?" Mom answers in a single word: "Bedtime."

(This is subtle humor here.)

Six kids in six years...

The only time the wife sees her husband is in bed...

Get it?

Never mind, you would've had to be there.

Cartoons are supposed to be funny. This one makes me feel like crying.

Sixteen years ago, as a young bride looking forward to marriage and parenthood, I felt so sure of the formula. After all, it was true. It must then be foolproof, right? I was convinced if I just did this (Family Home Evening every Monday night) and didn't do that (raise my voice unless the house was on fire) the whole marvelous adventure of raising children would be as assured of success as one of those paint-by-number landscapes I produced stacks of during my childhood. In Institute of Religion classes, exemplary teachers, revered for their willingness to put living the gospel above earning a living, taught the words of modern prophets, uttered over a hundred years ago, about the appropriate family size ("My wife had fifteen children...") and the sacred obligation of each woman to have as many children as she could, allowing only imminent death as an excuse to avoid pregnancy.

In the Relief Society meetings of our student wards, we idealistic young brides repeatedly taught each other the formulas for successful marriages and families, as we studied Daryl Hoole's *The Art of Homemaking* and Carol Lynn Pearson's poem "My Day-Old

Child." Delirious on the combination of such rhetoric and the hormones appropriate to eighteen-to-twenty-four-year-olds, we declared our willingness to do all we could to depopulate the premortal realms as quickly as possible and thus do our woman's part in bringing the Second Coming of Christ in a timely manner. We seriously believed He couldn't come until all the spirits "over there" were born, and any baby forced to be born into a non-LDS home was a shame we had to personally shoulder.

Twelve years and nine children later, I had even more invested in the hope the Millennium was imminent. As one child followed another in rapid succession, without a single sign of imminent death in either me or them, I came to realize parenting didn't have any formulas; success was not going to be a paint-by-number cinch.

Actually, it didn't taken me a dozen years to realize the rhetoric in the classroom lost something in the living. Within hours of bringing my very first newborn home from the hospital, though I hadn't wanted to admit it, I knew the truth—raising children wasn't anything like my former favorite creative pursuits, needlework and painting. In those efforts to produce something "lovely, of good report, and praiseworthy" my "raw materials" were inert, willing to sit still and let me shape them to fit my personal vision of success. The "raw materials" of motherhood, on the other hand, were anything but inert. No, they were definitely fluid—in more ways than one. They were full of self-will and determined to use their agency. Every time I thought I had my "picture" perfect, some of the "paint" decided to run.

Down in the trenches, I was losing my grip on the memory of those exemplary teachers who encouraged me with their examples and prophetic quotes. Where were they at three in the morning, when one child is throwing up, another has an earache, you've just found pornography under your fourteen-year-old son's mattress, and your husband has to get up and go to work in two hours? It was moments like these that taught me borrowed light doesn't last long in the trenches. Maybe I just needed to borrow some more. Maybe I needed to sign up for an Institute of Religion class at the community college. It was only a twenty-minute drive from my home. A half-hour there, an hour in class, a half-hour back. I'd only be gone for two hours. Surely, my husband could hold down the fort for two hours. The baby didn't nurse more often than that. Well, most of the time he didn't.

But, would more classes help? I listened and read enough, even cloistered as I was within the walls of my home, to know the emphasis in the Church was changing. Leaders and members alike were beginning to realize and expound for women a broader "measure of creation" than just biological; a broader scope of activity for the virtuous woman, one that included educational, civic, and creative pursuits. Going to class and listening to such words, at this stage of my life, would just rip me to shreds with envy and then with guilt for feeling the envy. Where were those alternatives when I was eagerly absorbing every word about motherhood eclipsing all other purposes in a woman's life? What in the world had I thought I was doing? What were my motives? Even dedication to God seemed a weak and shaky mooring for this overwhelming lifestyle I had so trustingly embraced. I felt like a plural wife when polygamy was renounced in the Church. I had given my all to this "principle" of bearing children, no matter what, and now it felt as if my whole culture had thrown on the brakes and left me and this principle behind.

"God!" I cried out in my heart and almost aloud, as I sat there in the dark. In all reverence I cried, "God, I can't go on. The borrowed light has turned to ashes."

The baby in me kicked and another contraction began. More false labor.

My attention wandered back to the movie.

Coming to an appropriate point in the lyrics of Popeye's immortal theme song, Robin Williams stops dancing down the boardwalk of the rickety seaside town, jumps off into the muddy street, plants his feet, and with a fist on each hip, belts out those words that are burned into the psyche of every child raised in the fifties:

> I yam what I yam, and that's all what I am. I'm Popeye…

Even if you were born after the abdication of Popeye and the Lone Ranger to Big Bird and Barney, you can fill in the last three words of Popeye's theme song. I definitely can. But not this time.

While everyone else around me—including my enchanted children—were seeing Popeye, my mind filled with the memory of a similar configuration of words, bringing instant recall of a movie set as dissimilar as could be from the one on the screen before me. From humid seaside to fiery desert mountain top, from Popeye to prophet (via Charleston Heston), my memory yanked me into what should have been a most hilarious transposition. In the present, my physical eyes looked upon Popeye; in my memory, I saw Moses confronting God, symbolized by a burning bush. Moses asked God for His name. Majestically, the voice of God is heard proclaiming the words, "I AM THAT I AM."

I heard harmony, symphonic harmony, in the statements of God and Popeye.

I AM THAT I AM.

Sincerely, without a single reservation, with unwavering commitment and integrity.

"I yam what I yam." Without a single second thought or doubt. Comfortable. At peace. What ya see is what ya get. I don't need to equivocate or apologize.

During the next several months following that moment in the theater, I became obsessed with an inner search. Being Christian, I am used to resolving paradox—wine coming from water, life from death, creation from chaos. Being a Mormon Christian only served to magnify the paradoxes to be pondered: Joseph Smith's exaltation of man's origin and destiny to the status of Godhood, contrasted with King Benjamin and Ammon's declaration of our "nothingness." I was used to being challenged to stand firm with a foot on two seemingly incongruous and conflicting opposites. After all, wasn't that what eternal marriage is all about?

But Popeye and God? Still, I could not deny I heard more harmony and less disparity between them that day in the theater than I heard within my disoriented and disheartened soul. I heard it and I knew it and I knew that God knew it. How could I deny it? But what did it mean?

$\mathcal{D}$

The birth of my baby, only a week overdue and blessedly routine, was hardly a distraction from my inner reverie. Though I looked sane on the outside, going about life in a rational way, inwardly I was continuously haunted by images of Popeye with a majestic booming voice, or was it by a burning bush with a swagger? Either way, those two fit together somehow, and I didn't fit with them. While nursing my baby in the dark silence of the night, I could feel myself blown about by every "wind of doctrine" about womanhood and woman's rights, woman's options.

Nearly a year later, shortly after the baby was weaned, I prevailed on my husband to take over for a weekend so I could get away. At first he was shocked when I told him I wasn't thinking of *us,* but of *me,* getting away alone. It was unheard of: a married Mormon woman with a small baby leaving her husband's bed to go somewhere without him or the baby? How could that be? Reluctantly, he listened to my plea for total solitude. I couldn't afford forty days and forty nights, but I had to go. He conceded.

I found a local motel room for the night, packed only my toothbrush, my journal and my scriptures, and drove away in our only car. My husband didn't walk me to the door. I left him in the kitchen, standing at the sink opening cans of pork-and-beans. On the sign taped to the cupboard, I crossed out "mother" and penciled in "father." I thought it might help him keep a cheerful attitude.

I was back home by ten the next morning. The motel didn't turn out to be a mount of transfiguration for me. If anything, it left me with more questions, not more answers. Why was I spending my life as a mother instead of in a career, multiplying my talents rather than my posterity? Because God wanted me to? I wanted these words to come out sounding like a statement, but they came out sounding like yet *another* question. What was I getting out of my motherhood? Fame, glory, honor, respect? No to all of those. Who was I pleasing? My husband. Not that he showed it. Myself? Not by any standard of peace or joy. God? Surely I was pleasing God at least, being so long-suffering and enduring. But then, hadn't He said something in the *New Testament* about not wanting us to be lukewarm; and again, in the *Book of Mormon*, about a grudging gift being like no gift at all? I had to admit, I felt pretty lukewarm, trudging out of bed most mornings. Did that make my motherhood a grudging gift?

My questions only brought the quicksand of more questions until my mind was reeling. In sheer terror of the abyss of non-personhood I seemed to be digging for myself, I had turned on the TV and resorted to watching pretend people solve pretend problems in half an hour. Eventually I crawled into the motel bed and fell asleep. There was no use wasting the opportunity for a whole night's sleep.

I worked hard to forget Popeye and Moses and the whole ridiculous thing. Several years later, after I had long since given up my hope for inner peace, concluding it wasn't something we ever accomplished in this life, I decided life was *supposed* to be a question, not an answer. A test, not a testament. Somehow, though, that didn't suffice—and feverish busyness was all that helped me forget it didn't. Then came the day when the busyness backfired; when, instead of keeping me from the abyss of unanswerable questions, it shoved me into it.

It was a day so much like all my other days. By 2:30 in the afternoon, it was almost more than I could stand. It was December. We were struggling financially, even more than usual, and Christmas was looking very lean. I had been sewing late into every night—clothes, stuffed toys, lap quilts, Cabbage Patch dolls—anything I could produce at home to save money *and stay busy*. I babysat other children three days a week to earn money for the sewing supplies.

Today was one of my "free" days. I had no extra kids to babysit, only my own three preschoolers. I got up early to drive my husband to work so I could keep the car to run errands and buy groceries. Running errands with three preschoolers challenges the imagination, believe me—first to Kinkos to copy some handouts for Primary, then to the cleaners to drop off my husband's suit, then to buy more yarn for the dolls' hair. However, it was the grocery shopping that was the killer. I talked my husband into letting me do it every two weeks instead of once a month as we had in the beginning of our marriage. A two-week supply was a little easier to get home. If I timed it just right, my school-age kids would be coming home and they'd help me unload the car.

Pushing two carts, one full of kids and one full of food, I got in line—ending up right behind Sally and Sam Something. I knew her from PTA. They were there at the store, with both their children, Susan and Shawn (who were born in Garanimals™—little replicas of their parents), who had just been chosen most obedient, clean, and *boring* children of the century. The four of them were just stopping off to stock their RV with a few extra goodies before they left on their two-week Christmas vacation to Disneyland, Marineland, and so on. I smiled and chatted, outwardly pleasant, but inside I was thinking, "May they get lost on Mr. Toad's Wild Ride or fall into a shark tank."

By the time I made it home, my jealousy was a full-blown case of pea-green envy. On top of that was the usual guilt for feeling jealous to begin with. Where were my values anyway? Damn, there was another one of those stupid questions. Great, now I had sworn and with a nursing baby at my shoulder, chewing on his fist and fussing. He'd just have to fuss, at least for a while. I'd be darned if I was going to nurse him again right now.

My preschoolers, in a state of delirium due to exhaustion, were running around at an ever-increasing rate of speed and producing an ever-increasing level of noise. They were throwing bread crusts from their late lunch of peanut butter sandwiches at each other. I was about to intervene but I only got out one small roar (the "house on fire" rule was abandoned long ago) before the phone rang.

It was Andrew, my fifteen-and-a-half-year-old, six-foot tall, 175-pound oldest child calling from school. Just from the sound of his voice I knew something was up. Where was that tone of teenage condescension? Through the shock of hearing him sound so amiable, I realized what he was saying. Did I remember that new friend he mentioned this morning—the one who just got a license to drive? Well, she (he hadn't mentioned it was a *she*) brought her mom's car to school today and was giving everybody a ride home after basketball practice. So, I didn't need to worry. Before I could say anything, he was gone. My "baby" was gone. And I shouldn't worry?

At that moment, my front door flew open, hitting the doorstop and bending it permanently into the wall. In stormed my grade-school kids in a total uproar. A snowball barreled past their heads and smashed into the split-entry stairs. For once, they weren't fighting each other. My eight-year-old turned to hurl an appropriate epithet back at the kid he'd just punched out on our front lawn. I couldn't decide whether to grab for the Ivory Liquid or look out to survey the remains. How could I have missed World War III, except for the phone, the baby, and the preschoolers? I stepped to the front picture window to get a look at the situation. The other kids were already running for home. Apparently, there was no serious damage, but that didn't even register. All I saw was my neighbor, the famous Patti Perfect, getting into her car. She had witnessed the whole thing.

Tears welled up in my eyes—the tears I had been holding back all day, all week, all month, all year. Stumbling to the nearest chair, I sat down and sobbed. The baby looked into my face and howled. The preschoolers stopped running around, and everyone stared at Mom.

Trying to catch my breath, I held the baby out to my oldest daughter, Karen. She took him in her arms. Mopping my face on my already stained coat sleeve, I pled with the others, "Go bring the groceries in, you guys." Hesitation. "I bought some fruit roll-ups." I watched as they dropped their bookbags where they stood and charged down the stairs toward the garage.

Karen put her hand on my shoulder and said softly, "It's all right, Mom. It's *all* right."

The truth in her words pierced my finally humbled and broken heart. No angel could have spoken to my heart with more power, more authority. She was right. Everything is *all* right. Everything. Patti Perfect, Sally Something, and me! Eleven kids in sixteen years, never-ending bills, home-made presents, nursing babies, painful, embarrassing moments, fifteen-year-olds growing up.

Recognizing that truth opened a flood gate into an even deeper storehouse of truth in my heart. Suddenly, I knew the answers to all those bottomless questions that had accumulated for so long. These answers came bursting into my mind in rapid succession, leaving no room for more questions. These were not borrowed truths. They were my own truths, my own answers, coming from somewhere deeper inside me than I had ever felt before.

Why am I doing this, living like this?

I haven't the slightest idea.

What am I getting out of this?

Absolutely nothing.

Who am I pleasing?

I couldn't care less.

I sat there in shock, staring blindly at the houses across the street. I knew the truth about myself. I was the world's biggest fraud. I'd been living a lie. I hung my head and closed my eyes against the light. I didn't want Karen to see the truth in my face. I heard her turn and carry the the baby into the kitchen.

But wait a minute. There was another answer coming from the depths of my being; another truth about *me*. It was coming from even deeper inside than the others. It rose to my consciousness. It was huge. It was absolute. It was turning my soul inside out.

And I wouldn't trade places with anyone in the world even if God himself offered me the chance.

I leaned back in the chair, trembling. I knew this feeling. This was birth.

I could plainly see now, I wasn't the victim of anyone else's expectations. I was right where I wanted to be, where I *chose* to be. All my past doubts were as dross and as stubble. I could feel them being consumed in the fire of my owned agency.

I opened my eyes. Then I stood up. I truly expected to be pounds lighter.

I looked around the room. Nothing had changed. The kids were emerging from the stairwell, hauling the groceries inside, laughing and shouting as they came. There was my neighbor driving past. I could see her looking towards our house, the front door was standing open. I stepped closer to the window, caught her eye and gave her a jaunty salute, Popeye style. Then I turned and spoke from my own burning bush.

"Come on, kids. Let's get the groceries put away before Daddy comes home."

I am what I am.

I AM THAT I AM.

Cloud

Where did you come from?
I watched you,
just now,
Materialize out of nothing,
Come out of nowhere.
Then I watched you
Disappear
The same way,
Back to where you came from.
Are you then, a wisp of nothing,
Like some say
I am.

Ask those who watch you
Unleash torrents of rain
On the earth.
Lives–
You give
And you take.
You have to be something
To do that.
Really something,
Sent by Someone.
But then you disappear.
You pass back into nothing.

Nothing?
I don't think so.

Families are Forever: the Promise

I was married at 18, sealed to my husband in the temple at 19, became a mother at 20, 21, 22, 24, twice at 26, again at 27, 28, 30, 32, 34, and the last time at 36. Was I crazy or consecrated? Paradoxically, I was simultaneously some of both.

> [there are] spirits waiting to take tabernacles, now what is our duty? to prepare tabernacles for them; to take a course that will not tend to drive those spirits into the families of the wicked, where they will be trained in wickedness, debauchery, and every species of crime. It is the duty of every righteous man and woman to prepare tabernacles for all the spirits they can... (Brigham Young, *Journal of Discourses*, 4:56)

> My wife has borne to me fifteen children. Anything short of this would have been less than her duty and privilege. (Elder George F. Richards, as quoted by Rodney Turner, *Woman and the Priesthood*, 121-122)

Words like these spoke to me, gave the truth in my heart a voice and words to call me, to seal me forever unto the work and glory of assisting God in providing as many of His children a physical body and a mortal probation as I possibly could. *Let's get the job done!* was my clarion cry for the first twenty-three years of my marriage and the motto driving my motherhood.

"If a job is once begun, never leave it 'til it's done. Be the labor great or small, do it well or not at all." My oldest, at two, could recite those words perfectly. They were gospel. They were *the* gospel. "Work, work, work while you may. There is no tomorrow, but only today."

Cooking, canning, cleaning, sewing, making love, having babies, going to church, developing family traditions, holidays, Family Home Evening, family prayer, scripture *reading*—all of it became a task to accomplish, another item on my list of "things to do today."

Unfortunately, with this focus, I heard the words, "Families are Forever" as a pronouncement, a prod, and sometimes, even a threat—anything but a promise. I added "Become a Forever Family" to my list and went at it with a singleness of purpose that left no room for any communication except my commands. I was convinced that my will was all that mattered. As far as I was concerned, we were going to be a "Forever Family" or go down trying.

Well, guess what?

Like a ship driven before a gale-force wind under too much sail—when less would have been the far wiser choice—my family, driven before my obsession to succeed, hit the hidden shoals of an unexpected crisis at full speed. We crashed. We went down. "My crew," as I had always defined them, were thrown into the sea, caught in the hidden currents of years of unexpressed feelings. We were alone—each of us—drowning in the very waves of pain and suffering I thought my piloting would avoid. I watched as some of my children, in their confusion, swam in the direction of the open sea, turning their back on the shore. Others swam in circles, dazed. Without good communication lines established, I found I could not reach them. They did not know how to relate to me as a counselor or comforter, only as a commander.

"Oh, Lord," I cried out in my anguish, "Look what I have done! Families can be forever, but I have wrecked mine! It is lost, destroyed, shattered,..."

From somewhere above and beyond and yet within the raging storm, I felt the Lord place His arms around me and turn my face back to the sea, inviting me to look. In amazement, I saw His power stretched out across the terrifying waves like a great network of lifelines, lying within easy reach of every one of my children as soon as they are ready to turn to Him. There is no reason for despair, only hope in Him and in His promises.

In direct assurance to my mind and heart, I seem to hear Him say, "You see, Colleen, the statement 'Families are Forever' was my mission statement long before it was yours. If you will look in D&C 50:42 you will find it stated most plainly. I intend to lose none that my Father has given me—I will feel after them, hoping always they will decide to give themselves to me. So let go, now, of the meaning of those words you have used as a lash to drive yourself and others. Receive them as *I* meant them: *as a promise.*"

Thus, today, as I deal with the choices of my children, I am able to remember that the words "Families Are Forever" do not mean that in the course of each family's history and each member's individual development, we must go around wearing matching tee-shirts, and behaving as if we're conjoined at the hip. Today, I realize it means that no matter how far they wander, there is an eternal bond between us that cannot be broken, no matter how far it is stretched. It is the sealing power of the Holy Spirit of Promise—even the Lord Jesus Christ's own promise.

Lies

You came,
Lying to me.
And I fell for it.
You wanted me to lie with you
And I did.
I lied to myself.
But I'm through now.
Through
And through.
I'm through
Lying
And calling it
Love.

Divorce – Act of Sin or Act of Repentance

*M*oses was a prophet of God. Doctrine and Covenants 1:38 assures us we can take Moses' words as if they were the Lord's own. If that is so, then who gave "the writing of divorcement" spoken of in Deuteronomy 24:1? Did Moses give it to the people or did God? It was God, acting through Moses, His prophet.

Why did God give the people the opportunity to divorce? The Lord supplied the answer to that question himself in Matthew 19:8 when He said, "Because of the hardness of your heart," and then ended His statement with the sorrowful words, "but from the beginning it was not so."

I hear in these words the Lord's own long-suffering, patient, and persuasive nature which He revealed to us in D&C 121:41 as the only foundation for genuine authority. His authority is perfect for the very reason that He is perfect in all the virtues ascribed to perfect administration in the priesthood, as listed in that verse (not only persuasion and long-suffering, but gentleness, meekness, love unfeigned, kindness, pure knowledge, etc.). I hear Him saying,

"Because I, God, know you are not perfect in your mortal state, we know you will not always make perfect choices, and so we have allowed Moses, our servant, to give you a way to repent, even from a choice as solemn as marriage. We would, however, that you always remember that in the beginning, marriage was meant to be eternal. We know, however, that mortal life is usually more real than ideal."

I hear the same "tone of voice" in this statement by President Joseph F. Smith, given in a conference address in 1914:

> If a man and woman should be joined together who are incompatible to each other it would be a mercy to them to be separated that they might have a chance to find other spirits that will be congenial to them. We may bind on earth and it will be bound in Heaven, and loose on earth and it will be loosed in Heaven. (*Messages of the First Presidency,* 4:327-32.)

While it is true some people might use this extension of God's mercy to justify their own selfish desire to shirk responsibility or to abandon a partner in order to pursue sin, it is also true that divorce may be a God-given opportunity to repent and begin again. Unfortunately for some of us, this gracious, loving, merciful understanding of divorce, based on acknowledgment and acceptance of human frailties and foibles, has rarely been openly discussed in our culture. Subsequently, some of us have been trapped in relationships in which we could never find favor in the eyes of our spouse. Thus, we were condemned to years of unending antagonism—a huge contrast to the kind of marriage that supports the highest degree of friendship and emotional, spiritual, and physical intimacy.

Maybe in fear that some people would take such "leniency" as an expression of approval or encouragement of divorce, the public position on divorce in LDS society has been unequivocally negative. Many of us experienced it as *scathingly* negative, equating divorce to the realm of evil and outright sin. Terrified of being defined as evil sinners, many of us are discouraged from taking this much needed act of repentance. Relationships of severe abuse—emotional, verbal, spiritual, physical, and even sexual—have sometimes been perpetuated by this absolute moratorium against divorce under any circumstances. I, for one, would have repented long ago if I had heard even a whisper of tolerance or understanding for this sorrowful and bludgeoningly painful option of last resort.

But, then again, maybe I wouldn't have. This discreet offer to admit my own foolish choices in my youth was actually there all along. However, in my pride and compulsive need to appear perfect, to fit in, to be accepted by others, I did not give myself permission to consider it.

Nevertheless, I now recognize divorce as a viable option—in fact, the *only* viable option for me. I accept my need to exercise this option. I humbly accept the fact that it's *okay* to be imperfect, to admit poor choices—even of this magnitude—and to believe and trust that Christ's power to redeem and repair is sufficient even for me and my children. I accept that it's okay in the sight of God if I let go and cease being responsible for the spiritual growth and maturity of another sovereign adult and that its okay to release both him and myself from my obsessive need to save him. I've come to realize there is only *one* Savior—and it's not me.

On Leper's Feet

Lord!
Heal me!
I cried
In pain.
My attempts to dress
My wounds
All vain.
He reached forth His hand
To reveal my ugly wounds,
Pull back
My dressing.
Again, I cried,
Lord!
Stop!

I must reveal your wound
To cleanse it, Heal it.

Unwilling,
I turned
And hobbled on
My way.

The Desert Shall Blossom as a Rose

*I*f there is one characteristic I have known in myself from my earliest memories, it has been an insatiable urge to comprehend and interpret this life I am living, to get all the understanding I can from this great adventure called Earth Life. As a child, I was ridiculed for this quality. When I was caught daydreaming, I was shamed for being "lazy" or "stupid."

"Get in here and *do* this right *now*!"

"Why are you always off playing?"

"You're always *goofing* off!"

"I can never find you; you're always out in the fields."

There was no one who recognized my day-dreaming as a gift for "seeing" and "pondering."

In my adult life I chose a partner who also made fun of and attacked the slightest sign of this quality in my personality. As long as I participated on the physical level of our "marriage," he was placated. But let me start to see past those surface experiences and try to talk to him about what I saw and he became derisive and belittling. Thus, I learned in adulthood to do what I had done in childhood—to hide this pondering part of me, even from myself.

Instead of developing my spiritual nature, I threw myself into the work of marriage and parenthood. In our culture we are reinforced and rewarded for accomplishing "work," or in other words, for producing and doing the things that show obvious results, *always doing*. Meanwhile, my true *being* was barely surviving in the cellar of my soul, due to neglect and starvation.

Fortunately, starvation does not result in death to an eternal spirit being. Instead, its result is dormancy—similar to the dormancy of many desert plants during years of severe drought. However, let the living presence of water touch these plants and the barren desert bursts forth again; it "blossoms as the rose."

Similarly, though the part of me that was my true gift from God and God's gift to the world in and through me *seemed* dead, it was only dormant. I found that out for sure several years ago, when life handed me a "season of the spirit." A season of the spirit is a time in our lives when there is nothing, absolutely NOTHING, left to cling to *except* the Spirit. Under such conditions—when all other sources of worth and results of my own hard work were stripped from me—the Living Water of Jesus Christ flowed into my soul and penetrated to a depth I had not known since the veil closed around me in childhood. I became as a little child again—believing and receiving the nourishment directly from the *living* Spirit of God. He became my living companion again, as He is to all little children.

In that spiritual awakening or birth, I saw the truth of how "unwhole" and untruthful I was all those years about my real self in order to retain the companionship of my marriage partner, to try and keep his "favor." I feared the loss of his companionship and support more than I feared the loss of my own deepest truth, my own deepest identity.

But when the Spirit of Truth, even Jesus Christ, touched that deepest truth in me, my spirit self burst into bloom. I could no longer deny it or pretend it didn't exist, that *I* didn't exist.

I said to my partner, "I am going to keep this beautiful blooming part of me out in full sight from now on. It is lovely, virtuous, of good report and praiseworthy. It teaches me to do good and love God (Moroni 7:13). I cannot hide it anymore. I *will* not hide it any more. I will not deny the gift of Christ's love for me or the presence of Living Water with which He nourishes me." My partner said, "I cannot live with such a person," and withdrew himself from me.

And now? Now I'm divorced and much to my surprise, I find my "season of the spirit" continues daily. I find myself acknowledging constantly that nothing—not spouse, not children, not other people's approval, not money, house or work—nothing short of God could be blessing me with so many unexpected and miraculous moments of insight and delight. His love is constantly with me. He is my Good Shepherd, my perfect husbandman and friend. It is my constant prayer that I will always need God this much, because I have found He responds to my *acknowledged* need. He is teaching me what it feels like to live in a partnership filled with mutual respect and adoration.

Because of this season of the spirit lived in the arms of Christ's love, I know that when I marry again it will not be at the cost of hiding and confining my truest self. God loves my truest, most honest identity. He loves the dreamer, the ponderer, and the writer in me. It is when I live in this mode that I live closest to God. I can see now that from the beginning the adversary was hard at work to destroy this part of me, because this is the "me" I was sent to earth to be. Today, it is the "me" that I AM.

Postscript: This essay was written in 1991. In January, 1999, I was blessed to marry again, this time to a man whose love of the Lord has magnified my joy and my freedom to be me. The greatest thing we have in common is our individual love for God. The second greatest thing we have in common is our enjoyment and adoration of each other. In this season of my life, the entire desert is a rose garden!

To Set at Liberty
Them That are Bruised

$\mathcal{A}$ few days ago, during my early morning scripture study, I came across these words in Isaiah:

> To appoint unto them that mourn in Zion, to give unto them beauty for ashes, the oil of joy for mourning, the garment of praise for the spirit of heaviness... (Isaiah 61:3)

And these words in Luke:

> The Spirit of the Lord is upon me, because he hath anointed me to preach the gospel to the poor; he hath sent me to heal the brokenhearted, to preach deliverance to the captives, and recovering of sight to the blind, to set at liberty *them that are bruised.* (Luke 4:18, emphasis added.)

As I read the precious words recorded by Luke, spoken by the Savior Himself, I wept at how much I have come to identify with each of those descriptive phrases: "the brokenhearted," "the captives," "the blind," and especially, "them that are bruised." How tender it is to me to realize the Lord Jesus Christ not only cares if we are stabbed and lacerated as He was, but even if we are "simply" *bruised*.

The word "bruised" fits so well for those of us who have lived with "invisible" violence. Like a bruise, this kind of damage is done just under the surface, hidden behind a thin skin of "fineness." Because the blood never quite leaks out, the wounds are easily hidden. They never get messy or obvious enough for anyone to know they're happening. However, I have learned *first-hand*, that God knows they're happening and He is not pleased. It was upon His own testimony directly to me, that I was given liberty to divorce myself from a life-time of absorbing the invisible violence of emotional and spiritual abuse.

The words in Isaiah, "To appoint [deliverance] unto them that mourn *in Zion*" also held a great key to my deliverance. Though I did a lot of mourning during the twenty-three years of my marriage, I was not doing my mourning *in Zion*, and thus could not receive the Savior's counsel or comfort in any complete way. I could not enter into Zion in those married years because I was serving the god of my own lust after the "perfect family," more than I was serving the God of Zion, even the Lord Jesus Christ. I was obsessed with the lie that I could somehow qualify *myself* to enter into Zion and find peace and rest in Her King.

Somehow, as I sat through years of church meetings, I became confused, thinking that spiritual self-reliance was as necessary and positive as temporal self-reliance. One of the most shameful situations I could be caught in as a Latter-day Saint, according to my perception of the messages I heard, was to be found needing anything beyond what I had the wisdom and foresight to provide for myself. The work ethic permeated my home and my life and slopped over into my spiritual life. I totally confused the work the sweat of my brow could accomplish with the price that only the sweat of *His* brow could pay. To me, it felt equally as shameful to need His Atoning Power or Grace as it did to admit I hadn't stored my year's supply of food. I suffered from the damning assumption that just as I was expected to "work out my own salvation" temporally, I was also expected to do so spiritually.

While others, the lepers and sinners, knelt at His feet, bathing them with their grateful tears, I thought I was supposed to be able to stand before Him straight and tall and hold out my clean hand with a proud heart...oops, I mean *pure* heart...and say, "Thank you, Lord, for your sacrifice. But guess what, I've kept myself so unspotted from the world that I only need a mere teaspoon of your Atonement. You see, I have been 'good' and have earned my salvation by my own efforts."

To put it more succinctly: I was convinced, despite King Benjamin's indicting question, "Are we not all beggars?" (Mosiah 4:19), that the most terrible fate I could ever suffer according to LDS cultural standards was to be a beggar of any kind.

Six years ago, life took a turn that made me realize Benjamin was absolutely right: we *are* all beggars. At least, I had to acknowledge that *I* am. No perfect record held out with clean hands and a proud heart was mine. On my knees with the lepers and the cripples, the divorcées and the single parents of troubled children, I drowned in the *depths* of humility and died a sort of death (as to the person I tried to be). In my own small way, I knew what it meant to drink a bitter cup that could not be passed from me; I knew a cross I could not come down from without abandoning God's Truth in me. With a pierced and broken heart, I sought the succor of Him whose heart had been pierced and broken for me.

Imagine my surprise when He turned my thoughts and my heart back to the Twelve Step principles He had led me to use several years before to overcome my compulsive need to hurt myself with food. Under the tutelage of His own Spirit, conveyed to me through the Holy Ghost, I searched the *Book of Mormon* from cover to cover—verse by verse—for these twelve principles or concepts. I found them confirmed on every hand, in every point! With renewed dedication, I took these steps again, one at a time, in order. I did so with real intent, with greater faith in Christ than I had ever experienced when addressing my eating behavior. Using these principles as a guide, I came closer and closer to the Savior. I examined my heart to its depths. I inventoried and admitted not only my negative behaviors, but also my negative thoughts *and beliefs*—the *roots* of my faithless, self-degrading and defeating choices I'd made over the preceding years. With fear and trembling, I brought all the "hidden things of darkness," all the lies I had harbored in my own soul, out into the light of His living reality as it was beginning to dawn in my heart and mind. I was sure His wrathful judgement would be waiting for me.

I will never be able to adequately describe the miracle of that moment of complete confession to Him, of complete admission of my unworthiness before Him. To my amazement, I did not perceive Him frown at me and tell me not to approach Him, unclean as I was. Instead, I perceived Him *smile* upon me and take me in His arms. He showed no concern, much less fear or judgment of my soiled, fallen condition. Instead, I felt His own light flooding into the dark places in my heart and mind, illuminating and cleansing them. One by one, as I allowed Him access to these hidden, wounded places, He changed my very disposition or inclination to think or do evil toward anyone—myself or others.

As is so beautifully described in Doctrine and Covenants 88:63, I found that as I drew nearer unto the Lord, He did indeed draw near unto me. My soul began to feel His peace. That peace that "passeth understanding," which is His hallmark, filled my soul. I was in His presence, not just occasionally, not just in moments of desperate emergency, but daily, sometimes hourly. Anytime I wanted to be still and reach out to Him in my mind, I found He was only a thought away. Through the instrumentality of the Holy Ghost, I began to recognize His voice, even as One crying in the wilderness (D&C 88:66) of my mind. His words were a guide to me. He counseled me in all things whatsoever I should do. As I learned to trust and live by every word that proceeded from Him, I found myself in His rest, in His spirit. In perfect assurance by His own witness to my soul, I learned I am precious in His sight. (D&C 88:68)

No number of affirmations on any number of tapes, or spoken any number of times before a mirror, can instill the kind of self-worth that *knowing the personal esteem of Jesus Christ for me* has instilled in my soul. Because of it, I do not function today from a place of "self-esteem," but from a place of knowing *God's* esteem. The actions I have taken to "take [myself] out of the slums,"[1] as President Benson put it, have been actions deeply grounded in God's esteem for me. I have come to know a part of the testimony of Jesus Christ that I never suspected—His testimony of me.

I cannot express how grateful I am for the ultimate freedom His testimony of me grants each new day, as I follow His commandments and seek to retain His witness. It is not a freedom from trials or even from mistakes, as I once thought it would be. Instead it is a freedom from the greatest fear I inherited in this fallen world—that somehow I am not enough and that I am not going to make it.

I *am* enough in the sight of God. I do not have to *qualify* for His love. In fact, I *cannot* qualify for it. *Nothing* I can ever do will equal His love for me. My efforts to please Him, to be like Him, do not come from my attempt to be worthy. My efforts, my obedience are motivated by this pure knowledge of *His* love for me. I know He loves me with a love that is a reflection of my *eternal* worth, and *He* will make sure I make it, if I keep coming back to Him, if I keep trying to live by His Spirit and His word, relying on His power to do so. I don't have to earn His Atonement. All I need to do is open my heart to Him and to His word to me, and abide— one day at a time—in the liberty wherewith *He* has made me free. (D&C 88:86)

[1](Ezra T. Benson, *Ensign*, July 1989, p. 4)

Please! Don't! Stop!

When we were little girls
We teased
About how if a boy
Ever kissed us,
We would yell,
Please...Don't...Stop!

Why is it
That today,
I feel exactly
That way
About God?

Touch Not the Unclean Gift, Neither to Give or to Receive It

...touch not the evil gift, nor the unclean thing. (Moroni 10:30)

*L*ift your eyebrow just a certain way. Use some other body language so subtle no one but me would notice it. Let your voice get ever so slight a tone in it, a tone that says "Okay, but I'm displeased, unhappy, sad, working on getting ticked, find you upsetting, find you boring"—and you'll have me chained to doing anything I can to please you. You see, I'm the kind of codependent that gets what I want by pleasing you. And what do I want? I want to be needed. In fact, I'm addicted to being needed. I'm addicted to being important. I'm addicted to being indispensable to you, whether you need a slave or a master. I'll be whatever you don't want to be. And if we're both codependent, as well as both addicts to some other behavior, we'll dance around each other, playing whatever role the other person doesn't want today.

If you get out of bed feeling like a victim, I'll rush right in to validate you by imposing my mind and will on you—so you'll feel better. If you get out of bed feeling like the victimizer, I'll not walk away from you and take care of my own sanity. I'll stay—and bow and scrape and sacrifice and suffer—so I will be needed in your need for someone to dominate on *that* day. And the next day? Who knows? That's part of the "rush" of it, the risk, the adrenaline high. It could be a day when I get to fix. Oh, what a savior I could be, if you'd just let me. Or it could be a day when I am the needy one and you get to "be strong." And around and around we go. Addict and codependent. Which role do you want this morning? The addict says, "It's everyone else's fault. Who can I blame?" The codependent sees that as a "help wanted" sign and jumps at the opportunity. The next day, they switch roles.

You see, *the truth is* addicts and codependents are caught up in the very same lie: That someone else is responsible. The addict says "You're responsible," and the codependent agrees, "Yes! Yes! I am. You're so right. If it weren't for me and my all-powerful self, you'd be different, everything would be better."

Which litany did you pick up this morning? Are you the addict, reciting how someone else is responsible for you being the way you are today, behaving the way you *have* to behave? Or are you the codependent, responsible for someone else's feelings and behavior today? *My son's a drug addict,... My daughter's overeating... It's all my fault. What can I do to make it right?*

Codependency is a displacement of accountability. It is a disorder of agency. It is a desecration of worship.

There are two faces to codependency. It either appears in the thought process as, "I'm in charge, I have to make everything right." Or it manifests itself as "I'm in charge, I made everything this messed up." It's ego run rampant on both counts, in both directions—whether running toward responsibility or running from it. It's a total lack of boundaries and lack of the humility to accept and tend to our own little piece of the "sidewalk." Instead we insist that one is responsible for the other's mess.

It is often asked, "So, do addicts cause codependency to happen, or do codependent people cause addicts to happen?" I believe they take turns enabling, more than causing, each other to stay in unhealthy patterns. They do a dance where both lead and both follow, simultaneously. They're one and the same creature, caught in a pattern of insanity that keeps both of them from owning their own life and their own mistakes and their own lessons. Both are caught in the cycle of playing God, instead of being still and knowing God. "God? God? How can I find time or attention to pay to God? I'm caught in this need to fix or avoid being fixed. Time, attention, energy, focus, consciousness—all given to what *he* wants, what *I* want. God will have to take a number and get in line."

Codependency is the underlying addiction of all addicts—in other words, every addict of any variety is also a codependent. I don't have to look at my own life very long or very deeply to see the truth of that statement for me. My urge to participate in my addictions—overeating, overspending, overworking, etc.—always begin because I feel scared or frustrated or abandoned or some other disturbing emotion in relationship to another person. And every codependent is also an addict. I can guarantee if you look closely enough at *any* codependent's private behavior, you'll find addictions practiced too.

Some people say it's hard to tell codependency from charity. Not really, not if you rely on your honest feelings to discern. Codependency comes with a price tag, *every* time. I'm doing this for you so you'll do or be something I need. Charity has no price tag. Charity is helping someone along *their* path, according to *their* plan, not mine.

"Touch not the unclean gift," is a warning to us all. Do not fall for the codependent's offer of binding help. You can tell whether you're receiving codependent service or charitable service every time by how you feel. If you feel like you're being bought sold out, taken for a ride—especially after seeking the Lord's counsel in your heart—it is a pretty certain sign you're being used while you're being "served."

"Give not the unclean gift" states the opposite but equally serious warning to avoid participation in the other side of the codependent dance. If you can honestly say you are not trying to control the other person, that you are hoping for no specific result in return for your help or effort for them, then you can know your gift is clean, freely given, not an act of covert judgment or manipulation. If, however, you find *the slightest* justification or rationalization in you to indicate you really do harbor a hope that your act of kindness will get this or that certain response—you are serving from a place of codependency. You are trying to control, to self-serve, to get what *you* want by being nice to the other person.

How can I tell what my motive is? By doing some serious and prayerful counseling with the Lord, inventorying—questioning and examining—my every urge to help another person. What would be His will for this person? If I help them in this way will it be a help to them or will it enable them to avoid or postpone the consequences of their own agency?

"What can I do to help?" if said with the unspoken thought, no matter how subtle, "so I can impress you, get you in my debt" or "so I can fix you, turn your life around, make you better" is codependency. It has "strings," an "ulterior motive," a hidden agenda.

In contrast, when I'm serving someone in the spirit of charity, I am doing it as a gift freely given. I might hope to see them come closer to the Lord, closer to the truth, let go of self-destructive ways, but none of that matters in my extension of help. Whether they change or not, my love and respect and enjoyment of *them*— that they exist, that I feel grateful and blessed to have them in my life—must not change. Only then can I know I am loving and serving with Christ's own love. Only then is my gift truly clean.

The Wonder Child Within: 'Our Life's Star'

Beneath the weight of mortality's veil of fears and tears, there dwells in each of us what I first heard John Bradshaw refer to as our "wonder child." He used the expression to describe our deepest and most true identity.

The wonder child is that portion of us that retains the unfathomable hope and the capacity for play of a secure and beloved child—the *child* of *God* the prophets try desperately to reawaken in us. Recovery from the lies of this world has brought the wonder child in me to consciousness lately. I find primarily, above all, my wonder child is a philosopher and a writer. Pondering through deep realities of life and sharing those thoughts in written words is my own humble version of Mozart's, Einstein's or Joseph Smith's passion. It is what I do when God and *good*—what feels *good, holy,* and *passionate*—finds expression in me.

We *all* have a wonder child, alive and waiting in each of us. As I watch and listen to others share their hearts in recovery circles, I wonder what each one *would* be if they just knew they *could* be. Not for money or for prestige, but for *fun*, for bliss, for joy—for

God. What is your wonder child? Do you know? Is he or she a dancer? An artist? A poet? A homemaker? A friend?

When you picture your wonder child spontaneously bursting into happiness and joy, what do you see him or her doing? Many of these things? Which one first?

I see my wonder child doing what I remember my real child self doing when I was five—sitting in the tall spring grass so characteristic of the Sacramento valley of the 1950's, pondering the wonder of it all—the grass, the bugs, the sky, the returning spring and cycle of seasons. Not dancing it out, or singing it out—but *thinking* it out. Feeling it, rejoicing in it as I ponder around it and through it—each delightful, delicious sensation and second of it.

I have come to know what Bradshaw was referring to when he talked of the wonder child. I believe he was describing that part of us "innocent from the beginning,"[1] that part of us that, as William Wordsworth puts it, "rises with us, our life's star."[2] Wordsworth goes on to describe us in our childhood as "trailing clouds of glory do we come from God, who is our home."[3]

This wonder child is truly our "life star." He or she is both a child and a fully mature eternal spirit. What a strange combination. A fully mature eternal spirit, probably millions and millions of years old (by earthly time) and yet, as we observe each one of us come through the veil, we see someone who comes as a child, pure, innocent, holy; at one simultaneously with their own primal truth and with all primal truth—that God is *in* and *through* all things (D&C 88:6), that all things work together for good (Romans 8:28), and that we all are that we might have joy (2 Nephi 2:25).

And so we come trailing clouds of glory and of truth, but the earth life that lies ahead is not designed to be a predominantly nurturing experience in which our deepest identity and all our purest gifts and talents will be recognized and encouraged. It is designed, instead, to be a challenge. It is designed to handicap us with a veil of forgetfulness. Wordsworth described it: "Our birth is but a sleep and a forgetting."[4] It is meant to, even as Wordsworth decries, close around us like "prison-house doors."[5] But why?

Why? we cry, as we look back at a lifelong struggle to recover our true self, our wonder child, from the "very chains and shackles and fetters of hell," (D&C 123:8) woven of the creeds of generations who have inadvertently inherited lies and in turn perpetrated them on us. Why? Why would a loving God send innocent, whole and holy children into such conditions of degradation and horrific challenge. As my wonder child within pondered this question one day, I saw in my mind's eye, as the eyes of my understanding were opened, the image of someone standing on the edge of a high cliff, preparing to dive into a dark sea, shrouded with mists thrown up by crashing waves.

I saw the truth that, like high divers, we leap from an incredible height in the eternal worlds where we once lived. We plunge deep into the thick, blinding sea of darkness called mortality. Now comes the fulfillment of God's benevolent purpose. What will we recognize about darkness and ourselves in contrast to it? Will the Light that we are respond to the Light of Christ, which is also resident in each of us (D&C 93:2), that calls to us to awaken from mortality's impact, to regain our true self—our wonder child? We live even now in the moment of hesitation, of question, of decision. All of heaven awaits our response to this test. Will we resurface? Or will we believe in and succumb to the darkness?

Struggling, straining, with every spiritual muscle aching and the need to breathe the breath of Life again, we find the One within that can empower us to swim for the Light above. In the depths of humility, admitting our own lost and fallen state without Him, we find firm bedrock to push off from.

We find ourselves as we find Him. Our wonder child, our life's star, our truest, most real identity is revealed to us and we know again the hope and joy of Christ's testimony to us: We are literal children of God, who is the *Father of Lights*.

Wonder of wonders! We are!

Light among Lights! We are! (James 1:17 & 18; D&C 88:50)

Let the truth prevail! Let the joy and rejoicing begin.

[1-6]Poetic quotes from "Intimations of Immortality" by William Wordsworth.

A Ramble of Your Own

While researching the personal essay for my thesis, I learned so many things about myself, about God. I have come to believe that writing, whatever the form, brings us closer to our true selves, closer to truth, closer to the divine. As I mentioned in the preface, I originally intended to leave this portion of the essay out. It was too scholarly, too dry, too unlike the others. But it still feels good to me to share it with you. And so, once again allowing the Lord to lead me along, not knowing the reason or the impact of this decision, I include it here.

Exploring the Tradition

The personal essay reminds us of our own and others' humanity. Its egalitarian nature comes from its intention not to attempt to constrain its subject or to subdue its audience, but to render as truly as possible the confluence of impressions and reflections which shape one's thought.[1]

In *The Art of the Personal Essay*, Phillip Lopate raises the question whether the personal essay is really a genre or merely a tradition.[2] I found in my own research, as Carl H. Klaus admits in the opening paragraph of his paper "Essayists on the Essay," that the MLA Bibliography is strangely silent on the essay, that its "boundaries, its terrain, its deep interior [is] a place few scholars had chosen to visit."[3] Klaus even goes so far as to propose it as an *"anti-genre,"* "whose distinguishing characteristic is its freedom from any governing aspect of form."[4] It demands and delights to take any form it chooses.

As I tried to trace the essay's history, I found that though the essay had some pretty illustrious names in its genealogy—Bacon, Montaigne, Stevenson, Woolf, to name just a few—it had almost disappeared from literary consideration by the middle of the twentieth century. In its resistance to method and form the personal essay nearly made itself extinct in literary circles. While fiction boomed in the last half of the century, nonfiction struggled to free itself from the image of a "bastard child, a second class citizen,"[5] by changing its name to the "paper," the "article," and even the "piece." The word "essay" was avoided "with horror," according to Joseph Kruthch.[6]

Then, as the influences of deconstructionist theory caused academics to look beneath historic assumptions of authority and objectivity, the truth had to be admitted. For all the abhorrence of the personal singular pronoun "I", *all* writing is situated, personal, and subjective. No matter how many established authorities I cite to make my point, it is still *my* point I'm making.

In the last several decades, as a new age of spiritual awakening has rebounded from the unfulfilled promises of humanism and the scientific method, even more energy has gathered to empower the blatantly honest "tradition" of the personal essay. Gradually, it has experienced a recovery that is phenomenal.

A Woman's Place in the Tradition

> Until recently, it was easier for women writers either to conceal themselves behind their characters in novels and plays or to fight against the tyranny of men in polemical treatises than to adopt the light irony or immodestly confessional self-exposure of the personal essayist... Fortunately the modern era has seen women writers adopting the essay form more and more, helping to revive it, transforming its concerns, and at times giving it a different sound.[7]

During that second semester, while I studied the traditional parameters of the personal essay, I also received my first exposure to feminism in a class on contemporary literary theory. I could not help but be struck by the similarities I heard between the characteristics of the personal essay and the feminine literary voice.

Scattered throughout Lopate's introduction I found the following descriptors for the essay: intimate, diverting, approachable; based on relationship and a sense of dialogue; it has a drive towards candor, self disclosure, ambivalence—changing positions and opinions at will. It struggles aloud for self-understanding, for honesty, in front of the reader. It honors and delights in the details of life, finding meaning in the most humble object, event, or circumstance. It does not present itself as the authority on anything except what the author is saying. It is an expression among equals. It is not being written to declare any conclusion or convince anyone, but simply to explore and share one's thoughts. It is an attempt to birth ideas and then let them go to find their own destiny, their own merit.[8] How familiar this all felt to my feminine soul.

As a woman just emerging from a multigenerational familial tradition of misogyny and silence, my heart leaped up! I felt like getting out a soap box and a bull-horn and shouting: Writing women, come forth! Come out from behind your fictional characters; come out from the cloistered confines of diaries, journals, and letters! Take up your own life, your own voice, your own opinion! Take up the personal essay!

Then I looked around and realized that women *are* taking up the personal essay, living and writing in the first person singular in ways that are both gratifying and disturbing to me. First I found and read the writing of the women Lopate named—Woolf, Fisher, Dillard, McCarthy, Rich. Then I sought newer voices and found Maya Angelou, Terry Tempest Williams, and Erica Jong writing autobiographical essays. Whetting my appetite on Woolf's and Dillard's book-length essays on the writing life, I went on to find further encouragement in the advice of Natalie Goldberg, Madeleine L'Engle, Brenda Ueland, and Burghild Nina Holzer. Upon reading the opinion of Lopate that inspirational and self-help books are really "collections of personal essays strung together,"[9] I realized I had read the work of women essayists for years—Catherine Marshall, Marianne Williamson, Clarissa Pinkola Estes, Melody Beattie, and Chieko Okazaki.

Essay Writing As a Therapeutic Tool

> The self-consciousness and self-reflection that essay writing demands cannot help but have an influence on the personal essayist's life....Thus the writing of personal essays not only monitors the self but helps it to gel. The essay is an enactment of the creation of self.[10]

My interest in English has always been a thinly disguised interest in the *source* of language—the human heart and mind. My driving passion is understanding *how* finding one's "voice"—especially through writing—facilitates a change that reaches to one's very core, that affects one's very nature. I know it happens. I have witnessed it and I have lived it. I've felt a visceral thrill when, in Rogers and Hamerstein's version of *The King and I*, Yul Brenner as the king plants his feet firmly, folds his arms across his chest and declares, "So let it be *written*. So let it be *done!*" When Hugh Nibley testifies that the ability to write is of divine origin and "remains and probably always will remain, the most effective means of binding time and space,"[11] something deep in my psyche stands up and takes note. I "burn" inside with that sense of knowing the truth of something I have no intellectual, rational reason to know.

I believe it is by this highly subjective sense of truth that all people live or die, and I have found no more effective means of getting down to this depth of honesty than the written word. According to Lopate, "The struggle for honesty is central to the ethos of the personal essay."[12] According to *God*, the struggle to align ourselves with truth is the ethos of our entire life.[13] As far as I can see, the process of essaying and living are one and the same.

When working as a lay-counselor with people recovering from abuse and addiction, I quickly introduce writing as a tool for both therapy and personal revelation. I watch individuals literally rescript their past and their future through writing essays about particular persons, places, circumstances or events of their lives— not changing facts, but *reinterpreting* the facts they recall. The essay proves to be an easier form of life-writing than journal or diary keeping. An essay has a beginning and end—a freeze-frame quality—that divides one's past into manageable, easier-to-process-size hunks.

I teach people to use quotes from sacred and secular texts as catalysts to instigate their own thoughts, feelings, meanings, applications. I call this "capturing," which is a process of exploring the internal landscape of their own truth. By exploring every thought, they can essay (test) their own feelings and insights as triggered by the text they are reading. This sense of dialoguing with the text has the effect of digesting and internalizing the concepts thus "discussed." It gives people practice in owning their own self, their own choices, their own responsibilities. To write a personal essay is an act of response. It demonstrates to a person that he or she has the ability to respond both to positive and to negative life events. I teach, both by example[14] and precept, the power of the personal essay as a vehicle to bring sanity and clarity to an otherwise confusing life experience. As Lopate states,

> So often the plot of the personal essay, its drama, its suspense, consists in watching how far the essayist can drop past his or her psychic defenses toward deeper levels of honesty.[15]

Essaying, this process of dropping past one's "psychic defenses," when done with sincere acknowledgment of the limits of human experience and the need of Divine grace and guidance, is actually the shedding of "the creeds of the [parents], who have inherited lies."[16] Essaying can thus be used to put people in touch with the source of *all* life and *all* light, even "the Spirit of truth."[17]

I have a great desire to continue writing and publishing in the genre of the essay, thus promoting its immense power for healing, for sanity, and for community. I hope my essays will carry messages that can be a bridge for others who are voiceless and frightened as I was.

The Personal Essay in Mormon Tradition

When Leslie Norris remarked to me in my first creative writing class that the personal essay is *the* genre of Mormonism, he also expressed his surprise that it doesn't receive more attention from us. I did not say then what I have come to believe—that of all the literary genres, the personal essay has the least hope of reaching full flower in the LDS culture because Mormon essayists will bloom only as we exercise one of the essay's greatest characteristics—to "walk around the elephant" and tell the whole truth. Nothing speaks to another's soul—body and spirit—more than speaking from my own soul. Nothing does more to ignite and fan the fires of honesty in another than to be honest myself. As children of God, creatures of light and truth ourselves,[18] we hunger for truth. The craving to be honest—to know and be known—is intrinsic in our primary, most primordial character,[19] though it may be buried beneath parental and societal paradigms of pretense and outright denial.

I also enjoy and find encouragement in the works of Mormon authors in other literary genres. For example, I long to develop and exercise in the personal essay the ability to "[explore] Mormon thought and culture in a critical but fundamentally affirmative way"[20] as does Professor Doug Thayer. I resonate to Carol Lynn Pearson's courage in autobiographical writing, not to mention her poetry and playwrighting. I cannot think of a more delightful, "full of light" voice than Hugh Nibley's. I long to emulate to the best of my ability his fearless combination of personal consecration and candor. Here again, is my ideal of the truth, the whole truth, and *nothing* but the truth.

According to Lopate, one of the attributes of a good personal essayist is that he or she is skilled at "locating a tension between two valid, opposing goals, or a partial virtue in some apparent ill, or an ambivalence in his own belief system."[21] I believe there is enough grace in the gospel of Christ—who did not reject a man's honest admittance of simultaneous belief *and* unbelief[22]—to allow such exploration of the discrepancy between our theology and our culture, our principles and ourselves.

In other words, humble and late to the vineyard as my efforts may be, I intend to add my voice to other Latter-day Saint writers who favor and even champion literary non-fiction in the form of the personal essay. I believe my life's experiences coupled with my education—graduate degrees in English and Human Development—gives me a powerful base from which to contribute to "a literature to match the high religious achievement of the Restoration Joseph Smith began."[23] I believe my familiarity with the inner fires of both martyrdom and rapture supplies me with the kind of dual or compound perspective Brigham Young described:

> We cannot obtain eternal life unless we actually know and comprehend by our experience the principle of good and the principle of evil, the light and the darkness, truth, virtue, and holiness, also vice, wickedness, and corruption.[24]

In this same spirit, it is my opinion that Latter-day Saints are capable of writing the greatest personal essays in the world—essays that have *redemptive* as well as recreational value. And so, dear reader, I invite you to put pen to paper and take a ramble of your very own. Follow the meanderings of your spirit. Discover your voice and the fire within.

[1]William Zieger, "The Personal Essay and Egalitarian Rhetoric," *Literary Nonfiction: Theory, Criticism, Pedagogy*, ed. Chris Anderson (Carbondale: Southern Illinois UP), 244.

[2]Phillip Lopate, *The Art of the Personal Essay: An Anthology from the Classical Era to the Present.* (New York: Doubleday, 1994), xxiii.

[3]Carl Klaus, "Essayists on the Essay," *Literary Nonfiction: Theory, Criticism, Pedagogy*, ed. Chris Anderson (Carbondale: Southern Illinois UP), 155.

[4]Ibid., 160.

[5] Chris Anderson, ed., *Literary Nonfiction: Theory, Criticism, Pedagogy,*(Carbondale: Southern Illinois UP), xviii.

[6]Joseph Wood Krutch, "No Essays, Please," *The Saturday Review of Literature,* 10 March 1951:18; quoted in Klaus, 162.

[7]Lopate, *Art.,* liii.

[8]Ibid.

[9]Phillip Lopate, "An Interview with Phillip Lopate," interview by John Bennion, *AWP Chronicle,* no. 4, vol.28 (February 1996): 1.

[10]Lopate, *Art.,* xliv.

[11]Hugh Nibley, *Enoch the Prophet* (Salt Lake City: Deseret Book, 1986), p.127.

[12]Lopate, *Art.*

[13]John 14:16–17; also Joseph F. Smith, *Teachings of the Prophet Joseph Smith* (Salt Lake City: Deseret Book, 1989), 150.

[14]I have edited and published a monthly newsletter called *Heartbeats* since 1991, providing an outlet for myself and others to share recovery centered writing.

[15]Lopate, *Art.,* xxv.

[16]Doctrine and Covenants 123:11

[17]Doctrine and Covenants 93:11

[18]Doctrine and Covenants 93:23

[19]Joseph Smith as recorded by Willard Richards; quoted in Andrew F. Ehat, ed., and Lyndon W. Cook, ed., *The Words of Joseph Smith* (Salt Lake City: Bookcraft, 1988), 340.

[20]Eugene England, "Mormon Literature: Progress and Prospects," *Mormon Americana: A Guide to Sources and Collections in the United States,* ed. David J. Whittaker (Provo, Utah: BYU Studies, 1995), 473.

[21]Lopate, *Art.,* xxvii.

[22]Mark 9:24

[23]England, 483.

[24]Ibid, 483.

Metaphorically

When I write
I am like Everest in hell
Melting down.
(Forget the snowball.)
A bottomless artesian well
Filled and flowing
Running o'er
Going on forever more.

When I write
I am like firecrackers going off
A thousand strong.
No, more.
Armageddon!
There's enough energy in me
To light the world
Or burn it to the ground.

It's all here inside me—
Counting down,
Counting down.

About the Author

Colleen Harrison, mother of twelve children and author of the best selling *He Did Deliver Me from Bondage*, has survived the death of her oldest daughter and the loss of her first marriage to addictive behavior. Drawing on the power (grace) of Jesus Christ, Colleen has completed a B.A. and an M.A. in English at Brigham Young University. While at BYU, Colleen combined courses in psychology, human development and creative writing to create a uniquely LDS version of narrative therapy. "Writing—in a journal, on the back of an envelope, anywhere—is one of the cheapest and most powerful forms of therapy a person can use to recover from addiction, compulsion, or any other earth-life challenges," Colleen maintains.

Currently, Colleen is pursuing a second Masters degree in Family and Human Development at Utah State University, in Logan, Utah. "Family and human development—that's what the restored gospel of Jesus Christ is all about—Eternal Family and Eternal Development." Strongly committed to both, Colleen continues to maintain the recovery the Lord has blessed her with through consistent, daily application of the Twelve Step principles as they correlate with the *Book of Mormon* and the gospel of Christ.

Colleen lives with her husband, Phil Harrison. They have a combined family of 17 children, 18 grandchildren, 3 cats and a dog. You may write to Colleen c/o Windhaven Publishing and Productions, P.O. Box 282, Pleasant Grove, UT 84062.

OTHER BOOKS BY COLLEEN HARRISON

He Did Deliver Me from Bondage

This best selling book is about awakening—becoming a whole new creature in Christ by putting God first, ridding one's self of pride and developing a relationship with God that is closer and sweeter than any other. It's about being delivered from the bondage of lies, recovered by the Spirit of Truth, Jesus Christ.

Written by a recovering compulsive eater, this book uses the *Book of Mormon* and the principles of the Gospel of Jesus Christ as they correlate with the Twelve–Step program to overcome compulsive/addictive behavior and other problems. Containing a series of twelve principles based on the Twelve Steps and supported by *Book of Mormon* scriptures and messages from our prophets, this book is used in many Twelve Step groups and for individual study.

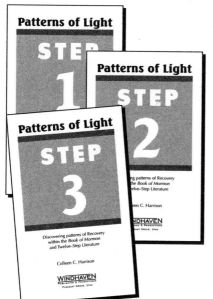

Patterns of Light

The Patterns of Light series inter-weaves selected LDS scriptures from the *Book of Mormon* with concepts from *Alcoholics Anonymous* (the AA "Big Book") and *Twelve Steps and Twelve Traditions* providing an in-depth study of the principles of recovery found in the Twelve Steps.

Scriptures are arranged in four sets of seven, creating a 4-week study of the Step. 5.5"x8.5"; paper cover.

To Order Books by Colleen Harrison

Send this order form along with check or money order (no COD's) in US dollars to the address below.

❏	1002	He Did Delver Me from Bondage (8.5" x 11")	$14.95
❏	1004	He Did Delver Me from Bondage (5.5" x 8.5")	$12.95
❏	1005	A Voice from the Fire	$9.95
❏	4101	Patterns of Light: Step One	$3.50
❏	4102	Patterns of Light: Step Two	$3.50
❏	4103	Patterns of Light: Step Three	$3.50

Tax   Please add 6.25% for books shipped to a Utah address.

Shipping   Add $2.00 ($4.00 CAN) for the first book and $.75 ($2.00 CAN) for each additional book to cover postage. (Overseas, call for rates.)

Send order to: Windhaven Publishing & Productions
P.O. Box 282, Pleasant Grove, UT 84062

Please send me the book(s) I have checked above. I am enclosing $_____ .

PLEASE PRINT: Date: _____

Name: _____

Address: _____

City, ST, ZIP _____

Phone: (_____) _____

Credit card orders may be place on-line at www.rosehavenpublishing.com.
Please allow 2—4 weeks for delivery. Prices subject to change without notice.